Getting Started

With

WordPerfect 6.0

For Windows

Getting Started With WordPerfect 6.0 For Windows

Kitty Daniels

Nancy Lynch Hale
Office Information Systems Department
Janet Smith
Pace Computer Learning Center
School of Computer Science and Information Systems
Pace University

Babette Kronstadt

David Sachs
Series Editors
Pace Computer Learning Center
School of Computer Science and Information Systems
Pace University

JOHN WILEY & SONS, INC.
New York / Chichester / Brisbane / Toronto / Singapore

Trademark Acknowledgments:

Microsoft is a registered trademark of Microsoft Corporation
Excel for Windows is a trademark of Microsoft Corporation
Windows is a trademark of Microsoft Corporation
Word for Windows is a trademark of Microsoft Corporation
Microsoft Access is a registered trademark of Microsoft Corporation
1-2-3 is a registered trademark of Lotus Development Corporation
WordPerfect is a registered trademark of WordPerfect Corporation
IBM is a registered trademark of International Business Machines Corporation
Paradox is a registered trademark of Borland International, Inc.

Portions of this text were adapted from other texts in this series and from Pace University Computer Learning
Center manuals.

ISBN 0-471-12068-5

Printed in the United States of America

10 9 8 7 6 5 4 3 2 1

Printed and bound by Malloy Lithographing, Inc.

Preface

Getting Started with WordPerfect 6.0 for Windows provides a step-by-step, hands-on introduction to *WordPerfect*. It is designed for students with basic PC and Windows skills who have little or no experience with *WordPerfect 6.0 for Windows*. Basic skills are taught in short, focused activities which build to create actual applications.

Key Elements

Each lesson in *Getting Started with WordPerfect 6.0 for Windows* uses eight key elements to help students master specific word processing/ss and *WordPerfect* concepts and skills and develop the ability to apply them in the future.

- **Learning objectives**, located at the beginning of each lesson, focus students on the skills to be learned.

- **Project orientation** allows the students to meet the objectives while creating a real-world application. Skills are developed as they are needed to complete projects, not to follow menus or other artificial organization.

- **Motivation** for each activity is supplied so that students learn *why* and *when* to perform an activity, rather than how to follow a series of instructions by rote.

- **Bulleted lists of step-by-step general procedures** introduce the tasks and provide a handy, quick reference.

- **Activities with step-by-step instructions** guide students as they apply the general procedures to solve the problems presented by the projects.

- **Screen displays** provide visual aids for learning and illustrate major steps.

- **Independent projects** provide opportunities to practice newly acquired skills with decreasing level of support.

- **Feature reference** at the end of the book allows students to have a single place to look for commands to carry out the activities learned in the book.

Stop and Go

The steps for completing each *WordPerfect for Windows* feature introduced in this book are covered in two ways. First they are described clearly in a bulleted list, which can also be used for reference. Then the steps are used in a hands-on Activity. Be sure to wait until the Activity to practice each feature on the computer.

Taking Advantage of Windows

Getting Started with WordPerfect 6.0 for Windows provides a balanced approach to using a Windows application. The use of the mouse, buttons, and icons for carrying out commands is emphasized. However, familiarity with the menus is developed so that students can take advantage of the greater options often available in menu commands.

Shortcut menus and shortcut keys are introduced when appropriate. The convenient **Feature Reference** at the end of the book summarizes menu commands and mouse and keyboard shortcuts for each of the features covered in the lessons. Students can use this both to review procedures or learn alternate ways of carrying out commands.

Flexible Use

Getting Started with WordPerfect 6.0 for Windows is designed for use in an introductory computer course. As a "getting started" book, it does not attempt to cover all of the features of the software. However, the topics included in later lessons allow instructors to provide opportunities for individualized or extra credit assignments or use the book in short courses focused specifically on *WordPerfect*. While designed to be used in conjunction with lectures or other instructor supervision, basic concepts are explained so that students can use the book in independent learning settings. Students should be able to follow specific instructions with minimal instructor assistance.

Data Disk

Data disks are provided to the instructors for distribution to the students. Many of the projects use files from the data disk so that the focus of the lesson is on the new skills being learned in each project. Initial projects require that students develop applications from the beginning, while later projects mix developing new applications with editing existing applications. Enough explanation and data entry is always included so that students understand the full application that they are building.

Acknowledgments

WordPerfect for Windows was written by three of us, but it represents the work and effort of many individuals and organizations. Babette Kronstadt provided energetic leadership and orchestrated the production of not only this book but all of Pace's books in the Getting Started Series. Nancy Treuer, Joe Knowlton, and Matthew Poli worked miracles with the layout and text formatting. Sylvia Russakoff, Sally Sobolewski, and Lynn Bacon shared their expertise unselfishly.

We received enormous institutional support from Pace University and the School of Computer Science and Information System (CSIS). In particular, much personal support and personal leadership for our work has come from the Dean, Dr. Susan Merritt. The faculty, staff and students of Office Information Systems Department including Dr. Alfreda Geiger and Professor Arlene August contributed useful comments to the concepts presented in this book.

From another perspective, this book is also a product of the Pace Computer Learning Center which is a loose affiliation of approximately 15 faculty and staff who have provided more than 7,000 days of instruction to over 60,000 individuals in corporate settings throughout the United States and around the world during the past nine years. Our shared experiences in the development and teaching of these non-credit workshops, as well as credit bearing courses through the Pace University School of Computer Science and Information Systems, was an ideal preparation for writing this book. In addition none of our books for Wiley would have been possible without the continuing support of David Sachs, the director of the Computer Learning Center.

We have received many invaluable comments and suggestions from instructors at other schools who were kind enough to review earlier books in the *Getting Started* series and offer their suggestions for the current books. Our thanks go to Jack D. Cundiff, Horry-Georgetown Technical College; Pat Fenton, West Valley College; Sharon Ann

Hill, University of Maryland; E. Gladys Norman, Linn-Benton Community College; and Barbara Jean Silvia, University of Rhode Island.

Our thanks also go to the many people at Wiley who provided us with the support and assistance we needed. Our editor, Beth Lang Golub, and editorial program assistant, David Kear, have been very responsive to our concerns, and supportive of all of the Pace Computer Learning Center's writing projects. Andrea Bryant was invaluable in her management of all aspects of the production of this book.

Last but not least, we would like to thank our families without whose support we could not have written this book.

Kitty Daniels
Nancy Lynch Hale
Janet Smith

December, 1994
White Plains, New York

Contents

3 ENHANCING TEXT   59

4 FORMATTING DOCUMENTS   85

5 WORKING WITH MULTIPLE PAGE DOCUMENTS AND GRAPHICS   111

6   MERGING   135

7   CREATING TABLES   159

Students and Instructors
Before Getting Started Please Note:

WINDOWS INTRODUCTION

Getting Started with WordPerfect 6.0 for Windows assumes that students are familiar with basic Windows concepts and can use a mouse. If not, instructors may consider using the companion book, *Getting Started with Windows 3.1*, also published by Wiley. Windows has a tutorial which can also help students learn or review basic mouse and Windows skills. To use the Windows Tutorial: 1) turn on the computer; 2) type: **win** or select Windows from the menu or ask your instructor how to start Windows on your system; 3) press the **ALT** key; 4) press the **H** key; 5) when the **Help** menu opens, type a **W**; and 6) follow the tutorial instructions, beginning with the mouse lesson if you do not already know how to use the mouse, or going directly to the Windows Basic lesson if you are a skilled mouse user.

STUDENT DATA DISKS

Most of the projects in this book require the use of a Data Disk. Instructors who have adopted this text are granted the right to distribute the files on the Data Disk to any student who has purchased a copy of the text. Instructors are free to post the files to standalone workstations or a network or provide individual copies of the disk to students. This book assumes that students who use their own disk know the name of the disk drive that they will be using it from. When using a network, students must know the name(s) of the drives and directories which will be used to open and save files.

SETUP OF WINDOWS AND WORDPERFECT 6.0 FOR WINDOWS

One of the strengths of Windows and *WordPerfect* is the ease with which the screens and even some of the program's responses to commands can be customized. This, however, can cause problems for students trying to learn how to use the programs. This book assumes that Windows and *WordPerfect for Windows* have been installed using the default settings and that they have not been changed by those using the programs. Some hints are given about where to look if the computer responds differently from the way it would under standard settings. If your screen looks different from those in the book, ask your instructor or laboratory assistant to check that the defaults have not been changed.

VERSION OF THE SOFTWARE

All of the screenshots in this book have been taken using Version 6.0a of *WordPerfect for Windows*. If you are using a different 6.0 version, the appearance of your screen and the effect of some commands may vary slightly from those used in this book.

Introduction

Objectives:

In the introduction you will learn how to:

- Start *WordPerfect for Windows*
- Identify the parts of the *WordPerfect for Windows* screen
- Work with the menu and dialog boxes
- Use the Button Bar

- Operate the Power Bar
- Change Views
- Use Help
- Exit *WordPerfect for Windows*

STARTING *WORDPERFECT FOR WINDOWS*

WordPerfect for Windows is a word processing application that is easy to use and powerful. A few of the easy tasks are inserting, deleting, moving or copying text, and checking for spelling errors. You can use the power of *WordPerfect* to accomplish more difficult tasks such as selecting fonts, changing layout, adding automatic page numbers, and mail merges. In learning to use *WordPerfect* you begin with the easy word processing tasks and gradually work your way up to the more powerful tasks.

Starting *WordPerfect* is the first task. Before you can start *WordPerfect*, you must start Windows. You begin Windows from the C> prompt by typing **win** and pressing **ENTER**. An hourglass ⏳ and copyright screen show while the computer works to bring up Windows. As the hourglass disappears, the Windows Program Manager appears.

In Program Manager the program group window for *WordPerfect for Windows*, WPWin 6.0, can appear either as an open window or as an icon. If you see the icon, move the mouse until the pointer is on the icon and double-click to open the window. To start *WordPerfect* with the WPWin 6.0 window open, move the mouse pointer to the WPWin 6.0 icon and double-click.

After you double-click the WPWin 6.0 icon, the Copyright screen for *WordPerfect* displays as the computer loads the program into memory. The Copyright screen displays the Version of *WordPerfect for Windows* stored on your computer. This book is based on *WordPerfect for Windows* Version 6.0a. You may notice differences between your screen and this book if you do not use the same version.

You must wait until the Copyright screen and the hourglass ⏳ disappear and the *WordPerfect* screen appears before you begin your work. As with all Windows applications, *WordPerfect* runs in a window.

NOTE: The steps for completing each *WordPerfect* feature in this book are covered in two ways. First they are described clearly in a **bulleted** list, which can also be used for reference. Then the steps are used in a hands-on *Activity*. Be sure to wait until the **numbered** instructions in the *Activity* to practice each feature on the computer.

To start *WordPerfect for Windows*:

- Turn on your computer.

- To start Windows, at the C> prompt type: **win**

- Press **ENTER**.

- In the Program Manager Window, you will see either the WPWin 6.0 program group window or icon. If you see the **WPWin 6.0** program group icon, move the mouse pointer on the icon and double-click. That will open the WPWin 6.0 program group window.

  WPWin 6.0

- In the WPWin 6.0 window, double-click the **WPWin 6.0** icon.

Activity I.1: Starting WordPerfect for Windows

1. Turn on your computer.

   The screen will display a variety of messages before displaying the C>prompt. The C> prompt may appear slightly differently, such as C:\>.

2. At the C> prompt, type: **win**.

3. Press **ENTER**.

   This command loads Windows into the computer's memory. An hourglass appears on the screen while Windows is loaded. When Windows has been loaded either the Program Manager screen is displayed, or the Program Manager icon appears at the lower left corner of the Windows desktop. The hourglass changes to the mouse pointer.

4. If the Program Manager is displayed as an icon, point to it and double-click.

   This action restores the Program Manager screen to its normal size.

WPWin 6.0

5. If the Program Manager screen is displayed, point to and double click on the **WPWin6.0** program group icon.

   This opens the WordPerfect 6.0 for Windows Application Window.

WPWin 6.0

6. Point to the **WPWin6.0** icon and double-click.

This action starts the WordPerfect program and displays the WordPerfect screen.

IDENTIFYING PARTS OF THE *WORDPERFECT* SCREEN

Before you start working on a document it is best to acquaint yourself with the parts of the *WordPerfect* screen. Figure I - 1 shows the parts of the *WordPerfect* screen. Some parts of the *WordPerfect* screen are identical to any other Windows screen. Table I-1 identifies the basic Window components of the *WordPerfect* screen.

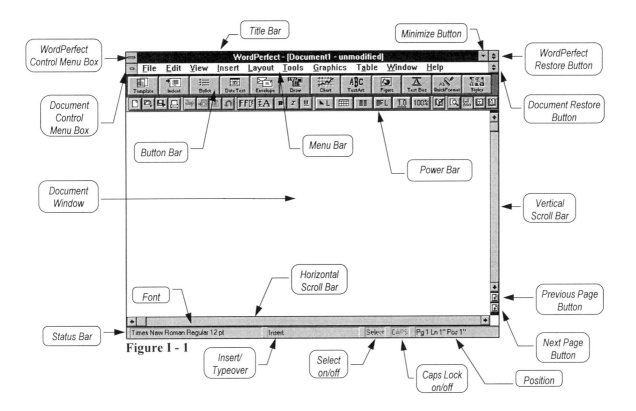

Figure I - 1

Table I-1: Window Components

Window Component	Definition
WordPerfect Control Menu Box	Displays a menu with commands for sizing and moving the *WordPerfect* window, switching to other applications, and closing *WordPerfect*.
Document Control Menu Box	Displays a menu with commands for sizing, moving, splitting, and closing the document window. Also the menu includes a command for moving the insertion point to a different document window.
Title Bar	Displays the name of the application, *WordPerfect*, and the name of the current document.
Minimize Button	Changes the *WordPerfect* window to an icon.
WordPerfect Restore Button	Returns the *WordPerfect* window to its previous size.
Document Restore Button	Returns the document window to its previous size.

Other parts of the screen are only seen in *WordPerfect*. Table I-2 identifies the *WordPerfect* components of the screen.

Table I-2: *WordPerfect* Screen Components

WordPerfect Screen Component	Definition
WordPerfect Menu Bar	Commands for working with *WordPerfect*.
Button Bar	Buttons used for quick access to editing features.
Power Bar	Icons used for quick access to features used most often.
Document Windows	Area for creating and editing the document.
Scroll Bars	Used for moving vertically and horizontally in a document.
Status Bar	Displays information about the current document: font, general status, select, caps lock, and position of insertion point.

As you move the mouse around to the different parts of the *WordPerfect* screen, the shape of the mouse pointer changes. The mouse pointer can show as an I-beam I, a single-headed arrow ↖, a double-headed arrow ↕, a four-headed arrow ✥ , a hand ☝, a question ?, or an hourglass ⌛. The shape of the mouse pointer changes depending on what is happening in *WordPerfect*. Throughout this book, mouse pointer changes will be noted as the different *WordPerfect* features are introduced.

WORKING WITH THE *WORDPERFECT* MENU

By making a menu choice you are telling *WordPerfect* what to do next. The ten menu command choices are File, Edit, View, Insert, Layout, Tools, Graphics, Table, Window, and Help. You can make menu choices using either the mouse or the keyboard. Some menu commands are carried out immediately. Other menu commands require more information from you before the command is completed. Any menu command followed by three dots (an ellipsis) will display a dialog box for you to read and specify how the command is completed.

To the right of some menu choices you will see a triangle. Any menu choice followed by this triangle opens another menu. To the right of some menu choices you will see a shortcut key or key combination. As an alternative to using the menu, the shortcut keys can be pressed. A plus sign between keys (such as **CTRL+N**) means that you need to hold down the first key while pressing the second. To the left of some menu choices you will see a check mark ✓. The check mark means that command is active. You can turn it off by clicking on the command. Figure I - 2 shows the **File** menu choices.

To make menu choices:

- Point to the menu command. The mouse pointer shape is a single-headed arrow ↖.

- Click the left mouse button to show the drop-down menu items.

- Point to the menu item and click the left mouse button.

- If a dialog box displays, read everything in the box and fill in each selection you need.

 KEYBOARD ALTERNATIVE: *Press the **ALT** key. The **Control** menu box to the left of the menu becomes darker to indicate the menu is active. Type the underlined letter of the menu command you want. Type the underlined letter of the menu item you want. If a dialog box displays, read everything in the box and fill in each selection you need.*

Occasionally you might open a menu and then realize that you are not ready to make a menu choice. This is not a problem. You can easily cancel from any menu using either the mouse or keyboard.

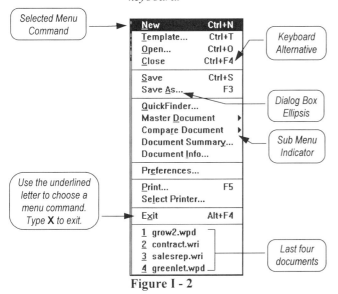

Figure I - 2

To cancel from the menu:

- Click the mouse outside the menu or press the **ALT** key.

WORKING WITH DIALOG BOXES

A dialog box is a special window containing choices that you select to tell *WordPerfect* how to carry out a menu command. As you work with different dialog boxes, you will notice common parts of dialog boxes. Table I-3 describes how to use each part of any dialog box with the mouse. Figure I-3 shows the **Print** dialog box.

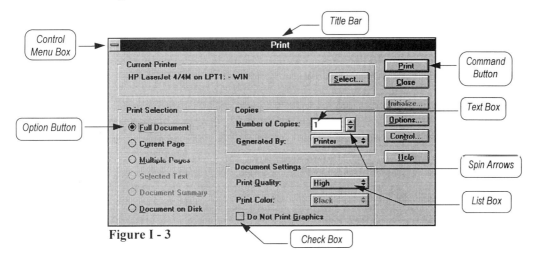

Figure I - 3

Table I-3: Dialog Box Components

Dialog Box Component	Use
Dialog Box Title Bar	Identifies the dialog box.
Control Menu Box	Double-clicking this box closes the dialog box.
Text Box	Place the insertion point in this box and type information, text, or numbers. To the right of some text boxes you see an up arrow and a down arrow known as Spin Arrows. By clicking on an up spin arrow, the number in the text box is increased. By clicking on a down spin arrow, the number in the text box is decreased.
List Box	Displays choices in alphabetical order. If there is a scroll bar to the right of the choices, use it to see additional choices.
Check Box	Click an empty check box to select it. Click a marked box to deselect it.
Option (Radio) Button	Click an option button to select it. Only one option can be active at a time.
Drop-down List	Click on the down-pointing arrow to display the list of choices.
Pop-up List	Hold down the left mouse button on the up-and-down arrows and drag to select your choice.
Command Button	Click on one to carry out its action. The OK **Command** button completes the command with the current choices. The **Cancel Command** button allows you to leave the dialog box without completing any choices.

USING THE *WORDPERFECT* BUTTON BAR

The *WordPerfect* Button Bar contains buttons for the features you use most often. When the mouse pointer is on a Button Bar button, an explanation of that button appears in the Title Bar. Click any button to use it. There is no way to use a button from the keyboard. Figure I - 4 shows the *WordPerfect* Button Bar. See Table I-4 for a description for each button on the Button Bar.

Figure I - 4

To make a Button Bar choice:

• Move the mouse pointer to the Button Bar button and click.

Table I-4: Buttons on the *WordPerfect* Button Bar

Button		Description
Template		Create a new document based on a template or ExpressDoc—**CTRL+T**.
Indent		Indent the current paragraph one tab stop—**F7**.
Bullet		Inserts bullets and numbers into the document.
Date Text		Insert the current date at the insertion point—**CTRL+D**.
Envelope		Create an envelope.
Draw		Create a graphic with WP Draw.
Chart		Create a chart with WP Draw.
TextArt		Create TextArt and special effects.
Figure		Retrieve a graphics image into a figure box.
Text Box		Create a text box.
Quick Format		Apply current fonts/attributes or paragraph styles to other text.
Styles		Create, edit, and select styles—**ALT+F8**.

OPERATING THE *WORDPERFECT* POWER BAR

The Power Bar allows easy access to the most frequently used text editing and layout features. As with the Button Bar, you must use the mouse to select a button on the Power Bar. When the mouse pointer is on a button, its description shows in the Title Bar. Figure I - 5 shows the Power Bar, and Table I-5 describes each button on the Power Bar.

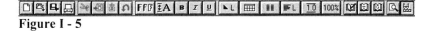

Figure I - 5

To make a Power Bar selection:

• Move the mouse pointer to the **Power Bar** button and click.

Table I-5: Buttons on the *WordPerfect* Power Bar

Power Bar Button	Description
New Document	Create a new document in a new window — **CTRL+N.**
Open	Retrieve an existing document into a new window— **CTRL+O.**
Save	Save the current document—**CTRL+S.**
Print	Print a document—**F5.**
Cut	Move or cut selected text or graphics to the Clipboard —**CTRL+X.**
Copy	Copy selected text or graphics to the Clipboard— **CTRL+C.**
Paste	Insert the Clipboard contents at the insertion point— **CTRL+V.**
Undo	Reverse the last change made to the document— **CTRL+Z.**
Font Face	Change the typeface of printed characters.
Font Size	Change the size of printed characters.
Bold Font	Turn on bold font — **CTRL+B.**
Italic Font	Turn on italic font — **CTRL+I.**
Underline Font	Turn on underline font — **CTRL+U.**
Tab Set	Specify the types and positions of tab stops.
Table Quick Create	Click and drag to create a table.
Columns Define	Specify the number, type, and size of columns.
Justification	Align text in document.
Line Spacing	Specify line spacing for current document.
Zoom	Zoom document in or out.
Speller	Check for misspelled words, double words, irregular capitalization—**CTRL+F1.**
Thesaurus	Display synonyms and antonyms for a word— **ALT+F1.**
Grammatik	Check document for proper grammar and spelling— **ALT+SHIFT+F1.**
Page Zoom Full	Select the Page view, zoom to full page size.
View Button Bar	Hide the current Button Bar.

Activity I.2: Using the WordPerfect Menu and Power Bar

1. Move the mouse pointer to different parts of the screen without clicking.

   When the mouse pointer is on the document editing area, it shows as an I-beam. When the mouse pointer is on the title bar, menu bar, Button Bar, Power Bar, scroll bars, or status bar, it shows as an arrow.

2. Move the mouse pointer to each button on the Button Bar and Power Bar.

   When the mouse pointer is on a button, a description for that button shows in the title bar. Read the description for each button.

3. Move the mouse pointer to the **FILE** menu choice and click the left mouse button.

   The File Menu opens. There is an ellipsis after the Print choice.

4. Move the mouse pointer to the **Print** choice and click the left mouse button.

   The Print dialog box opens as shown in Figure I-3. Identify the different parts of the dialog box. Is the Current Printer name shown in Figure I-3 the same as you see on your screen?

5. Click on the **Close** button in the **Print** dialog box.

   The dialog box closes and does not print a document.

6. Type: **Power Bar**

7. Press **ENTER**.

   The insertion point moves to the next line.

8. Click on the **Underline Font** button on the Power Bar.

   The Status Bar shows the Font Name underlined.

9. Type: **Power Bar**

   The text appears underlined.

10. Press **ENTER**.

11. Click on the **Italic Font** button on the Power Bar.

    The Status Bar shows the Font Name in italic.

12. Type: **Power Bar**

    The text appears both italic and underlined.

13. To close the document, double-click the **Control** menu box for the document window.

    A message appears that asks, "Save changes to Document1?"

14. Click on the **No** button.

    The text you typed in and the message disappears. A blank document screen displays.

CHANGING THE VIEW

WordPerfect has the capability of displaying many different screen views other than the one displayed when you first start *WordPerfect*. You can control screen changes by making a **VIEW** menu choice, or sometimes *WordPerfect* automatically makes screen changes for you. Throughout this book any screen changes will be noted as the corresponding *WordPerfect* feature is introduced.

After starting *WordPerfect*, if you open the **VIEW** menu you see that the default view settings are Page, Button Bar, Power Bar, Status Bar, and Graphics. Whenever you are working with *WordPerfect* and you find the screen display confusing, restore the default view settings to return to a familiar display. You may find it unnecessary to change views as you begin to learn *WordPerfect*. As you continue to learn and use the more powerful features, then changing the view becomes more useful. Figure I - 6 shows the open View menu, and Table I-6 summarizes the views offered by *WordPerfect*.

Table I-6: Views in *WordPerfect*

View	Description
Draft	Information displays more quickly as you move through your document. Some features such as headers, footers, watermarks, and certain formats do not appear.
Page	Information displays in full WYSIWYG (what you see is what you get). On the computer screen only part of the entire page is shown.
Two Page	Two consecutive pages are displayed side-by-side.
Zoom	Information displays to a specified size on screen (does not affect the size of text when printed).
Button Bar	Displays the Button Bar when active. Hides the Button Bar when off.
Power Bar	Displays the Power Bar when active. Hides the Power Bar when off.
Ruler Bar	Displays the ruler bar when active. Hides the ruler bar when off.
Status Bar	Displays the status bar when active. Hides the status bar when off.
Hide Bars	Hides the menu, scroll, ruler, power, button, and status bars when active for a clean screen. To display the bars again, press **ESC** or **ALT+V** and select **Hide Bars**.
Graphics	Hide graphics to edit text more quickly. Graphics print even if the screen hides the graphics.
Table Gridlines	Displays gridlines for speeding up editing. When gridlines are hidden, the computer slows down displaying table lines.
Hidden Text	Displays hidden text when active. Hides hidden text when off.
Show ¶	Displays codes wherever there is a space, a hard return, a tab, or an indent.
Reveal Codes	Displays formatting codes in your document when active. Hides formatting codes when off.

Description of the View menu
command displays in the Title Bar

Active View commands
preceded by check mark

Page, Button Bar, Power Bar,
Status Bar, and Graphics are
default view choices.

Figure I - 6

USING *WORDPERFECT* HELP

At any time you are working with *WordPerfect*, you can bring Help information up on your screen. The Help information shows in a window that has a Menu Bar and several buttons to make Help easy to use. There are numerous topics in Help.

There are three different ways to start Help: One way to start Help is to make the last choice in the *WordPerfect* Menu Bar. Table I-7 describes the choices in the Help Menu.

Another way to get Help is to press the **F1** key. The Help topic shown is context-sensitive to what you were working on when you pressed **F1**.

A third way to get Help is to press **SHIFT+F1** to activate Help: What Is? The mouse pointer changes to a question mark pointer. Now if you click on any part of the screen or make any menu choice, Help concerning what you clicked on shows.

Table I-7: *WordPerfect* **Help Menu Choices**

Help Menu Choice	**Description**
Contents	A list of all online Help sections.
Search for Help	Get online Help for a specific topic.
How Do I	Instructions for performing common tasks.
Macros	An online macros manual.
Coach	A list of mini-tutorials to coach you through a feature you are using.
Transition Advisor	A list of features, terminology, and keystrokes for *WordPerfect for Windows*.
Tutorial	Step-by-step tour of using *WordPerfect* basics.
About *WordPerfect*	Information about the license number, version of *WordPerfect*, and available memory.

On a Help screen, if you see information that is green and underlined with a solid line, it is a topic. If you move the mouse pointer to the topic, the shape of the mouse changes to show as a hand 🖑. By clicking the mouse on a topic, you go to that Help topic.

On a Help screen, if you see information that is green and underlined with dots, it is a term. By clicking the mouse on a term, you see a definition displayed in a box. After you read the definition, click on the term again to close the box. Figure I - 7 shows the Using Help topic in *WordPerfect* Help.

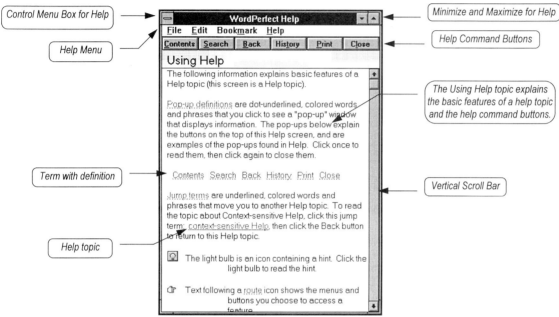

Figure I - 7

To start *WordPerfect* Help:

- Choose **HELP** in the *WordPerfect* menu.

- Select a **Help** menu item.

To start context-sensitive *WordPerfect* Help:

- As you are using a *WordPerfect* feature and need more information about the feature, press **F1**.

To use Help: What Is?:

- Press **SHIFT+F1**.

- Click on a part of the screen or drag to a menu item.

Activity I.3: Using WordPerfect Help

1. Press **SHIFT+F1**.

    The mouse pointer changes to show a question mark.

2. Click on the **New** button on the Power Bar. It is the first button.

*The WordPerfect Help window opens to the New Document topic. Read this information.
You will start a new file in Lesson 2.*

3. Click on the **Contents** button in the Help window.

   A list of Help topics appears.

4. Click on the last topic, **Using Help**.

   *Your screen shows the same information as Figure I - 2. Read the information using the
   Scroll Bar to see all the text.*

5. Click on the **Control** menu box for the Help window.

   *The **Control** menu choices appear.*

6. Click on **Close**.

   The Help window disappears from the screen.

EXITING *WORDPERFECT*

When you complete your work in *WordPerfect*, you should exit or close *WordPerfect* and
Windows before you turn off your computer. Never turn off the computer when *WordPerfect* for
Windows is on the screen.

If you lose power while *WordPerfect* is running, the next time you start *WordPerfect for
Windows* you may see a message that "Timed backup Document1 exists." Document1 is the file
that was open when the power went out. You have three choices: Rename, Open, or Delete.
Choose **Rename** to save this backup file. Choose **Open** to see Document1 to determine if you
want to save this file. Choose **Delete** if you are sure you don't want this backup file.

Do not exit *WordPerfect* if you need to return to use it later in the day. Since *WordPerfect* is
a Windows based application, at any time you are using *WordPerfect*, you may switch to another
Windows application. It is unnecessary to exit *WordPerfect for Windows* to use such software as
Quattro Pro or Paradox for Windows. At any time while using another Windows application, you
can switch back to *WordPerfect*.

To close *WordPerfect*:

- Double-click the top left *WordPerfect* **Control** menu box.

  The dialog box shown in Figure I - 8 appears.

- If you have not saved your work, you will be prompted with three choices: Yes, No, or
  Cancel. To save changes to the file, choose **Yes**. To exit without saving changes to the file,
  choose **No**. If you choose **Cancel**, you can continue working in your *WordPerfect* document.

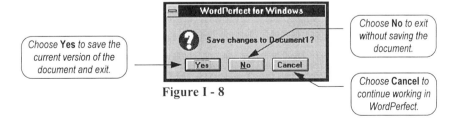

Choose **Yes** to save the current version of the document and exit.

Choose **No** to exit without saving the document.

Choose **Cancel** to continue working in WordPerfect.

Figure I - 8

To close Windows:

- Double-click the **Windows Control** menu box.

- Answer **OK** to the prompt, "This will end your Windows session."

If you have not saved your work, you will again be prompted with the three choices, Yes, No, or Cancel. To save changes to the file, choose **Yes**. To exit without saving changes to the file, choose **No**. If you choose **Cancel**, you can continue working in Windows.

KEY TERMS

Button Bar
Check Box
Command Button
Dialog Box
Document Control Menu Box
Document Window
Drop-down List
Insertion Point
List Box
Maximize Button
Menu Bar
WordPerfect Control Menu Box

Minimize Button
Option Button
Pop-up List
Power Bar
Restore Button
Scroll Bar
Status Bar
Text Box
Title Bar
View

Lesson **Creating and Printing a Simple Document**

Objectives

In this lesson you will learn how to:

- Create a simple document
- Work with word wrap
- Save, close, and open a file
- Move around a document
- Insert text in a document

- Delete text in a document
- Typeover text in a document
- Resave a file
- Print a file

PROJECT: CREATING A SIMPLE DOCUMENT

Some word processing procedures are basic to creating any document. Entering text, making changes, saving the document as a computer file, and printing the document are important procedures used when creating any document with *WordPerfect*.

Throughout this book you will be creating several documents for a cooking school named Creative Cookery. This school offers a wide variety of cooking classes. The project begins with a phone call from Mary Anderson to Creative Cookery requesting information about classes. Several activities guide you through all the necessary steps to create a letter from Creative Cookery to Mary Anderson. Figure 1-1 shows the first draft of the letter.

While creating the letter, basic procedures for working with *WordPerfect* will be performed. First, you will enter the text. Then you will save the document. Next, you will make changes to the document. After the first draft of the letter is completed, you will make several changes before the final version is ready and printed.

ENTERING TEXT

When you first start *WordPerfect*, the Title Bar displays WordPerfect - [Document1 - unmodified]. This title indicates that you may begin typing the new document. As you type from the computer keyboard, do not worry about making mistakes. If you do notice you are making a mistake as you type, press the **BACKSPACE** key as many times as necessary to erase the mistake. Any other mistakes can be corrected after you complete the typing.

All documents are assigned format settings. The default settings assigned by *WordPerfect* are 8.5 by 11 inch paper, one inch top, bottom, left, and right margins, single line spacing, and Times New Roman 12 point font. In Lessons 3 and 4 you will learn how to change these format settings.

When you enter text with the computer keyboard, you will work with uppercase letters, blank lines, and word wrap.

Creative Cookery
Yaphank Commons
Yaphank, NY 11980

Today's Date

Ms. Mary Anderson
123 Elm Street
White Plains, NY 16666

Dear Ms. Anderson:

Thank you for your inquiry about classes offered at Creative Cookery. The enclosed material should give you a better understanding of our cooking school, the classes that we offer and the schedule for the next two sessions.

We are proud of our reputation for putting the student first. We feel that this attitude is one of the most important contributors to our success and to the success of the students we teach. We are equally proud of our staff. Each chef on our staff has worked at one or more of the top-rated restaurants, both in the United States and Europe.

The Creative Cookery classes for the next session are filling quickly. To register for the next session, please call (516)555-1234 as soon as possible and ask for Gregory. I will be extremely happy to assist you and answer any of your questions. Thank you for your interest.

Sincerely,

Gregory Zaleta
Vice President

GZ

Enclosure

Figure 1 - 1 Document, First Draft

Uppercase Letters

To type one uppercase letter, hold down the **SHIFT** key while pressing the letter key. To type several uppercase letters, first press and release the **CAPS LOCK** key. Now whatever letters you type are uppercase. To turn Caps Lock off, press the **CAPS LOCK** key again. The **CAPS LOCK** key affects only letters, not numbers or punctuation keys. Only use **CAPS LOCK** for more than one uppercase letter.

Blank Lines

Press the **ENTER** key to include a blank line. If you are at the beginning of a line, press the **ENTER** key once. If you are within a line of text, press the **ENTER** key twice.

Word Wrap

Word wrap is a feature that makes it unnecessary to press the **ENTER** key at the end of each line. *WordPerfect* will know when your text reaches the right margin and will automatically move you to the next line.

It is important not to press the **ENTER** key at the end of each line so that word wrap takes place. Pressing **ENTER** key at the end of each line causes editing problems. Only press the **ENTER** key when you want to begin a new paragraph or when you want to end the line before the text reaches the right margin, as when you type an address in a letter.

Activity 1.1: Entering Text

Now you will begin entering the text for the letter from Creative Cookery to Mary Anderson. The letter will be set up in *Full Block letter style*, which means that all parts of a letter, sender's address, date, recipient's address, salutation, body, closing, and signature, are typed at the left margin. Refer again to Figure 1 - 1 for the finished version of the first draft.

1. Start *WordPerfect for Windows*. Follow the instructions in the Introductory Lesson, if necessary.

    A blank document screen displays. When the mouse pointer is in the document area, the Title Bar shows, WordPerfect - [Document1 - unmodified]. The insertion point blinks in the document area and the Status Bar displays Pg 1 Ln 1" Pos 1" as the position of the insertion point on the page. Ln 1" represents the position from the top of the page. Pos 1" represents the position from the left edge of the page.

2. To start typing the name of the cooking school with Uppercase C, hold down the **SHIFT** key as you press **c**.

3. To complete the name of the school, type : **reative Cookery**

    The insertion point moves as you type. The status bar changes to show the new position of the insertion point.

4. Press the **ENTER** key.

    The insertion point moves to the beginning of the next line, Pg 1 Ln 1.2" Pos 1".

5. Type: **Yaphank Commons**

6. Press the **ENTER** key.

7. Type: **Yaphank, NY 11980**

    The return address is completed

8. Press the **ENTER** key twice.

    A blank line is created after the address.

9. Click on the **Date Text** button on the Button Bar.

    WordPerfect automatically types in today's date at the insertion point.

10. Press the **ENTER** key four times.

    Three blank lines are created after the date.

11. Press the **ENTER** key after typing each line of Mary Anderson's address. Type:

Ms. Mary Anderson
123 Elm Street
White Plains, NY 16666

The inside address is completed.

12. Press the **ENTER** key twice.

A blank line is created after the inside address.

13. Type: **Dear Ms. Anderson:**

The salutation is completed.

14. Press the **ENTER** key twice.

A blank line is created after the salutation.

15. Now type the first paragraph as shown in Figure 1 - 1 *without* pressing the **ENTER** key at the end of each line. Press the **ENTER** key twice at the end of the paragraph.

Word wrap fits the right amount of text on each line of the paragraph to fit from the left to the right margin. There is a blank line after the paragraph. Figure 1 - 2 shows the present appearance of the screen.

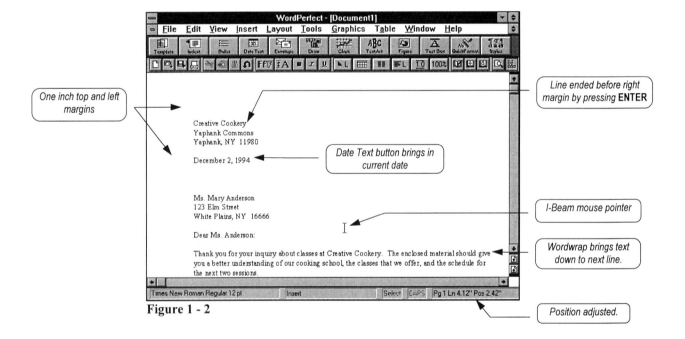

Figure 1 - 2

16. Type the remaining paragraphs as shown in Figure 1 - 1. Press the **ENTER** key twice at the end of each paragraph.

The beginning of the letter is scrolled off the top of the screen. WordPerfect displays only a portion of a page at a time. You can move to any part of the letter, and after you complete typing and saving the letter, you will learn ways to move the insertion point.

17. Type: **Sincerely,**

18. Press the **ENTER** key four times.

Space is allotted for the signature.

19. Type: **Gregory Zaleta** and press the **ENTER** key.

20. Type: **Vice President** and press the **ENTER** key.

21. Type initials, press **ENTER** twice, and type the enclose notation.

The closing is completed and all the text is entered.

SAVING A DOCUMENT

Saving is one of the most important computer procedures you will perform. Text that you type in but do not save will be lost when you exit from *WordPerfect* or turn off the computer. When you save your text, it is stored on disk so that you can use it whenever it is needed.

A name is assigned to a document so that when you need to use it again you can ask for it by name. The name you give a file is restricted by certain rules. Filenames are limited to eight characters. No spaces are permitted within the filename. *WordPerfect* automatically assigns a period and the letters **wpd** for the end of the filename. Uppercase and lowercase letters can be typed for the filename; however, the name is not case sensitive. So, if you type **budget** for the file name, *WordPerfect* will show that as **budget.wpd**. It is important to name files in such a way that when you see the filename later, you can recall what is in the file.

The document can be saved to any drive or directory on the computer. If you do not specify which drive or directory, *WordPerfect* stores the document in the default document directory. The initial default document directory is **c:\wpwin60\WPDOCS**.

> **REMEMBER:** Read the bulleted list that follows, but do not actually perform the steps until you reach Activity 1.2.

To save a new document:

- Click the **Save** button ![Save button] on the Power Bar.

- The **Save As** dialog box appears as shown in Figure 1 - 3.

- Type a name for the document in the **Filename** text box.

- To save to the default document directory, do not make changes to the drive or directory. Select a different drive or directory to store the file somewhere other than the default.

- Click the **OK** button.

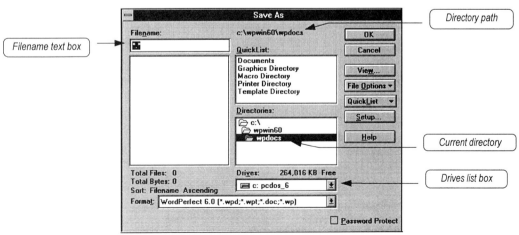

Figure 1 - 3

Activity 1.2: Saving the Document as a File

Even though the letter to Mary is not in final form, you will save the document now. So far, the text that you entered is only temporarily stored in the computer's memory. Once the text is saved, it is stored permanently on a computer disk. Saving documents frequently safeguards against loss of information.

1. As you work with this book, files may be saved to the data disk or on the hard drive of the computer. If you do not know where to save files, ask the appropriate person now which drive and directory to use. Fill in this blank with the answer.

   _____

2. If you will be saving the file to the data disk, place the data disk in the computer. Some computers have only one drive for working with disks named Drive A. Other computers have two drives for disks, named Drive A and Drive B. If your computer has two drives, make sure you insert the data disk in the drive shown in the blank above. If you will be saving to the computer's hard drive, it is unnecessary to use the data disk.

3. The letter you typed in shows on the screen. Click the **Save** button on the Power Bar.

   *The **Save As** dialog box appears on screen. It is important to read each dialog box as you use it. In the **Filename** part of this dialog box, you see *.* highlighted, and the insertion point blinking at the end of the highlighting. Since the insertion point shows in the **Filename** box, it is the active area of the dialog box. This means that if you type now the letters will appear in the Filename box. The name of the current Drive and Directory shows to the right of the **Filename** area and all the directories for that Drive are listed.*

4. Type: **ltrandem**.

   CAUTION: *Do not press the **ENTER** key after you type in the filename. Pressing the **ENTER** key finishes the dialog box in the same way as clicking the **OK** button does. At this point you have not assigned the Drive or Directory for storing the file. You must complete all the choices in the dialog box before you press the **ENTER** key or click on **OK**.*

   The *.* disappears and ltrandem shows in the Filename text box. The insertion point is blinking after the name. The ltr in the name is to indicate that the file is a letter, the ande is the beginning of the last name, and the m is the first initial. Since WordPerfect organizes filenames alphabetically, all the letters will show in a group. In the letter group, the filenames will be listed alphabetically by last name and then first initial.

5. Open the **Drives** list box and click on the name of the Drive that you entered noted in the blank at the beginning of Activity 1.2.

   The list of directories changes to show what directory names have been set up for use on the active drive.

6. If you are saving the file to the hard drive, click on the name of the Directory that you entered in the blank at the beginning of this Activity 1.2.

   *The current drive and directory reflect the choices you just made and shows under the **Save As** in the Title Bar of the dialog box. Figure 1 - 4 shows how the **Save As** dialog box appears if you are saving to Drive A.*

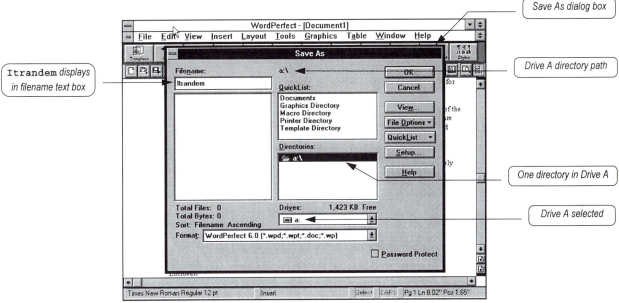

Figure 1 - 4

7. Click on **OK** or press the **ENTER** key.

    The light on the computer drive to which you are saving the file illuminates as the computer stores the document. An hourglass may show briefly to indicate that the computer needs time to save the file. When saving is complete, the drive, directory, and filename are displayed in the Title Bar, such as [a:\ltrandem.wpd - unmodified]. If you do not see the filename in the Title Bar, move the mouse pointer to the document area of the screen and look again.

From this point on, if the book does not specify which drive and directory to use, assume that you should use the one you entered in the blank line at the beginning of Activity 1.2.

CLOSING A FILE

Any document that you work with in *WordPerfect* is in a document window. Although *WordPerfect* allows you to work with several documents at the same time, the best procedure to follow when using *WordPerfect* is to close a document window when you are finished working with that document. After you close the file, it will not show on the screen. If you saved the document, it is stored on disk.

If you attempt to close a document that has not been saved, *WordPerfect* will give you a chance to save the file so that you do not accidentally lose the document. If you close the document and do not save it, you will not be able to open that file again.

To close a file:

*   Double-click the **Control** menu box for the Document Window.

*   If *WordPerfect* displays the question, as in Figure 1 - 5, **"Save changes to filename?"**, click on **Yes** to save the file.

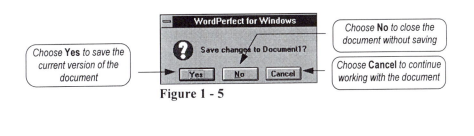

Figure 1 - 5

Activity 1.3: Closing the Letter

The first draft of the letter to Mary Anderson is saved to disk with the name **ltrandem.wpd**. By closing the file you will clear it from the screen.

1. Double-click the **Control** menu box for the Document Window

 CAUTION: *If you double-click the **Control** menu box for the WordPerfect Application Window, you will exit from WordPerfect. The **Control** menu box for the Document Window will either be directly below the WordPerfect **Control** menu box or below the Power Bar. If the Document Window is maximized, its **Control** menu box is directly below the WordPerfect **Control** menu box. If the Document Window is restored, its **Control** menu box is below the Power Bar.*

The document area is blank and the Title Bar shows [Document1 - unmodified]. The Status Bar displays Pg 1 Ln 1" Pos 1". The computer is ready for you to begin work on a new file or to open a saved file.

Opening a File

Any file that has been saved can be opened. The **Open File** dialog box is displayed in Figure 1-6. When it is open, the file is shown on the screen in a document window. The open file can be edited.

To open a file:

*   Click on the **Open** button [ ] on the Power Bar.

    *The **Open File** dialog box appears (Figure 1 - 6).*

*   If you do not see the file that you want to use, change the drive and directory to where the file is stored.

*   From the list that is displayed, choose the filename by clicking on it.

*   Choose the **OK** button or press the **ENTER** key.

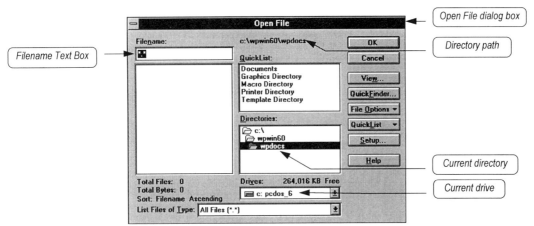

Figure 1 - 6

Activity 1.4: Opening the Letter

Now you will edit the first draft of the letter to Mary. In order to work with that document again, you must open it to bring it back up in a window on the screen.

1. Click on the **Open** button on the Power Bar.

    *The **Open File** dialog box shows on the screen. It names the active drive and directory. The files in that drive and directory are listed alphabetically.*

2. Select **ltrandem.wpd** by clicking on it.

    *The filename highlighted in color is the active file among all the files listed. Figure 1 - 7 shows the **Open File** dialog box if you are opening the file from Drive A.*

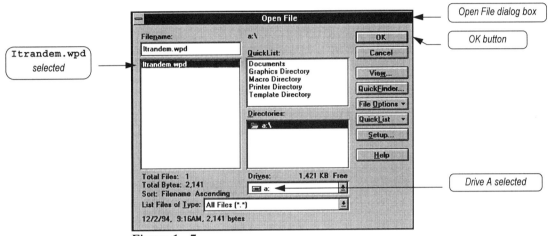

Figure 1 - 7

3. Click on the **OK** button.

    WordPerfect displays the file on screen. The Title Bar displays the name of the file.

Whenever you are unable to finish all the activities in a project, save and close the document. When you want to continue with the project, open the file.

MOVING AROUND THE DOCUMENT

Ease of editing is one of the best reasons to use *WordPerfect* for word processing. For editing, you must move the insertion point to the text you want to change. Either the mouse or the keyboard can be used to move the insertion point.

Distinguishing the mouse pointer from the insertion point is crucial. The mouse pointer changes shape as you move the mouse to different parts of the screen. When the mouse pointer is in the text area of the screen, it shows as an I-beam. The insertion point always shows in the same way, as a blinking vertical bar. The insertion point is the active position in the file. As you work, the position of the insertion point determines where editing takes places.

Scrolling the screen may be necessary to see the part of the document that you want to edit. As you scroll the screen, the insertion point does not move. For some editing work, you will scroll first and then move the insertion point.

To scroll the screen:

•   Click the down arrow ↓ on the scroll bar to move down one line at a time.

- Click the up arrow ↑ on the scroll bar to move up one line at a time.

- Click the scroll bar above the scroll box to move one screen up.

- Click the scroll bar below the scroll box to move one screen down.

- Drag the scroll box up or down to scroll quickly.

- Click the **Next** [icon] or **Previous Page** [icon] buttons to scroll one page at a time.

To move the insertion point:

- Move the mouse pointer to the position where you want to work. Use the scroll bars to show the part of the document with which you want to work.

- Click the mouse.

- Once you see the insertion point blinking in the right position, you may move the mouse pointer to a different position on the screen. The mouse pointer does not need to be at the same position as the insertion point to edit.

Table 1-1: Insertion Point Movement with Keys

Key	Movement
→ (RIGHT ARROW)	One character to the right
← (LEFT ARROW)	One character to the left
↓ (DOWN ARROW)	One line down
↑ (UP ARROW)	One line up
CTRL+ →	One word to the right
CTRL+ ←	One word to the left
HOME	Beginning of the line
END	End of the line
PAGE UP	Up one window
PAGE DOWN	Down one window
CTRL+HOME	Beginning of the document
CTRL+END	End of the document

Activity 1.5: Moving the Insertion Point

Take some time now to try each of the different ways to scroll the screen and move the insertion point. Look to see how the box on the scroll bar and the Ln and Pos on the status bar change with each try. To edit effectively, you must be comfortable scrolling and moving the insertion point.

EDITING TEXT

There are various ways to edit with *WordPerfect*. Inserting, deleting, and typing over text are basic to making many editing changes.

Inserting Text

WordPerfect makes it easy to add text to your document. As you add in new text, the text in the document is rearranged to adjust for the new text. The new text can be automatically inserted or can be typed over existing text. By looking at the status bar, you will see what mode for inserting text is active. If the status bar displays *Insert*, anything you type will be added to the document at the insertion point position. If the status bar displays *Typeover*, anything you type will replace the existing text. As you start *WordPerfect*, *Insert* mode is active.

To insert text:

- Move the insertion point to the position where you want the new text to be inserted.
- Type the new text.

Activity 1.6: Inserting Text

As you begin to proofread the letter to Mary, you notice several mistakes. Mary's address is 123 North Elm Street. You wanted to start the second paragraph with a sentence about how long the cooking school has been in business. Gregory Zaleta always uses his middle initial, A. The second sentence is missing a comma. To make these editing changes you will insert text.

1. Look at the status bar. If you see *Typeover*, press the **INSERT** key once. Continue when you see *Insert* on the status bar.

2. Move the insertion point so that it blinks at the beginning of the word **Elm** in Mary's address. *Figure 1 - 8 shows the insertion point positioned to insert North to the street address.*

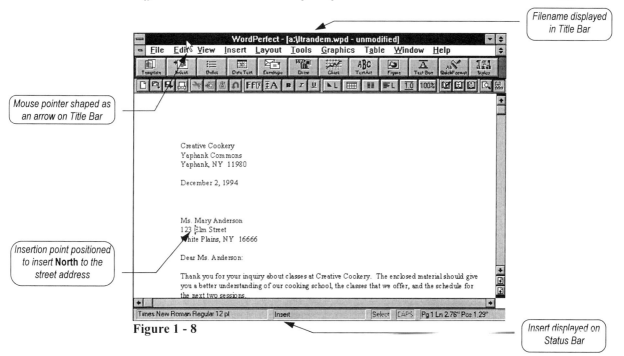

Figure 1 - 8

3. Type: **North**
4. Press the **SPACE BAR.**
5. Move the insertion point to the beginning of the second paragraph.
6. Type: **Creative Cookery has been teaching students in the Long Island area since 1960.**
7. Just as you do after any sentence, press the **SPACE BAR** twice.
8. Move the insertion point to the beginning of **Zaleta** in the closing.
9. Type: **A.**

10. Press the **SPACE BAR**.

11. Move the insertion point to the end of the word **offer** in the second sentence.

12. Type: ,

Deleting Text

Either the **BACKSPACE** or **DELETE** key can be used to delete one character at a time. The **BACKSPACE** key removes the character to the left of the insertion point and the **DELETE** key deletes the character to the right of the insertion point. Be careful to press the key without holding it down; otherwise, you might delete more than you wanted.

To delete with the BACKSPACE key:

- Position the insertion point to the right of the character to delete.
- Press the **BACKSPACE** key once for each character to delete.

To delete with the DELETE key:

- Position the insertion point to the left of the character to delete.
- Press the **DELETE** key once for each character to delete.

Activity 1.7: Deleting Text

As you continue to proofread the letter to Mary, you notice more mistakes. In the third paragraph, you want to refer to **Greg** rather than **Gregory** and eliminate the word **extremely**.

1. Position the insertion point between the **y** of **Gregory** and the period at the end of the second sentence of the third paragraph (Figure 1 - 9).

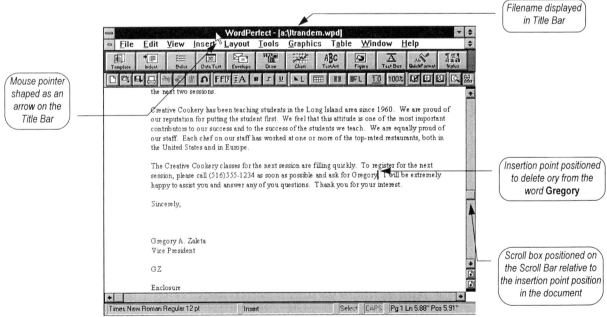

Figure 1 - 9

2. Press the **BACKSPACE** key three times.

3. Position the insertion point before the word **extremely** in the third sentence of the third paragraph.

4. Press the **DELETE** key repeatedly until the word **extremely** and the space that follows it are deleted.

Typing Over Text

For some editing changes it is better to work in *Typeover* mode rather than *Insert* mode. To change *WordPerfect* to *Typeover* mode, press the **INSERT** key. The status bar shows *Typeover* when it is active. Now the text you type at the insertion point replaces the existing text. To return to *Insert* mode, press the **INSERT** key again.

To typeover text:

• Position the insertion point where you want to replace text with new text.

• Press the **INSERT** key to turn *Typeover* on.

• Type the new text.

• Press the **INSERT** key again to turn *Typeover* off.

Activity 1.8: Using Typeover

In matching Mary's address to the phone message you received about her call, you realize that her address is **123 North Elm Avenue** (not Street) and that the zip code is **10606**.

1. Position the insertion point before the **S** of **Street** in Mary's address.

2. Press the **INSERT** key.

*The status bar displays **Typeover** as an indication that as you type, the new text will replace (typeover) existing text. Figure 1 - 10 shows the insertion point positioned for this editing change, and the status bar displays **Typeover**.*

Figure 1 - 10

3.   Type: **Avenue**

The street address is corrected to show as 123 North Elm Avenue.

4.   Position the insertion point between the **1** and **6** in the zip code in Mary's address.

5.   Type: **060**

The zip code is corrected to show as 10606.

6.   Press the **INSERT** key again.

WordPerfect returns to Insert mode.   The status bar shows Insert.

7.   Compare the document on your screen to Figure 1 - 11. Make any needed editing changes to match the documents.

RESAVING A FILE

Any changes you make to a document after you save the file are temporary. For the computer to remember the changes, you must resave the file. As a *WordPerfect* user it is best to follow this advice: save early and save often. Saving every 10 to 15 minutes safeguards against accidental loss of large portions of documents.

WordPerfect responds differently when you are saving a file you have already named and saved. When you use the **Save** button on the Power Bar or choose **FILE/Save** to resave, *WordPerfect* saves the file without displaying the **Save** or **Save As** dialog box. *WordPerfect* assumes that you want to save the file with the same name to the same drive and directory.

To resave a file:

•   Click the **Save** button on the Power Bar.

Activity 1.9: Resaving the File

The editing changes you made to the letter will be saved. The same name, **ltrandem.wpd**, will be used as the file is saved the second time.

1.   Click the **Save** button on the Power Bar.

The light of the drive to which you are saving the file flashes briefly. When saving is complete, the title bar displays the word unmodified after the filename.

PRINTING A FILE

After you have typed, edited, and saved a document, you will want to perform another basic word processing task, printing. You can choose how WordPerfect prints your file by making choices in the **Print** dialog box. If you make no choices in the **Print** dialog box, one copy of the entire file will print. Figure 1-6 displays the **Print** dialog box.

Saving the file before you print is very important. Occasionally a problem develops as the file information is transferred from the computer to the printer. If you do not save before you print, you risk losing file information.

Creative Cookery
Yaphank Commons
Yaphank, NY 11980

Today's Date

Ms. Mary Anderson
123 North Elm Avenue
White Plains, NY 10606

Dear Ms. Anderson:

Thank you for your inquiry about classes offered at Creative Cookery. The enclosed material should give you a better understanding of our cooking school, the classes that we offer, and the schedule for the next two sessions.

Creative Cookery has been teaching students in the Long Island area since 1960. We are proud of our reputation for putting the student first. We feel that this attitude is one of the most important contributors to our success and to the success of the students we teach. We are equally proud of our staff. Each chef on our staff has worked at one or more of the top-rated restaurants, both in the United States and Europe.

The Creative Cookery classes for the next session are filling quickly. To register for the next session, please call (516)555-1234 as soon as possible and ask for Greg. I will be happy to assist you and answer any of your questions. Thank you for your interest.

Sincerely,

Gregory A. Zaleta
Vice President

GZ

Enclosure

Figure 1 - 11 Document, Final Version

To print a file:

- Save the file.

- Check the printer to make sure it is ready to print: the power is on, the printer is on-line, and the paper is ready.

- Click on the **Print** button  on the Power Bar.

- Click the **Print** button in the **Print** dialog box to print one copy of the entire file

Activity 1.10: Printing the Letter

You have completed entering the text, saving the file, making editing changes, and resaving the file. Now you are ready to print.

1.   Prepare the printer for printing.

2.   Click the **Print** button on the Power Bar.

     *The **Print** dialog box is displayed as in Figure 1 - 12. It is set to print the full document and the number of copies is one.*

3.   Click the **Print** button in the **Print** dialog box.

     *The **Print** dialog box disappears. On screen a message informs you that WordPerfect is "Preparing Document for Printing." The letter prints and the file stays on screen. WordPerfect's default settings show on the printout, 1 inch left, right, top, and bottom margins, single line spacing, and 8.5 by 11 inch paper size.*

4.   **Close** the file by double-clicking the Document **Control** menu box.

     *The document window is blank. The title bar displays **[Document1 - unmodified].** The first project is finished.*

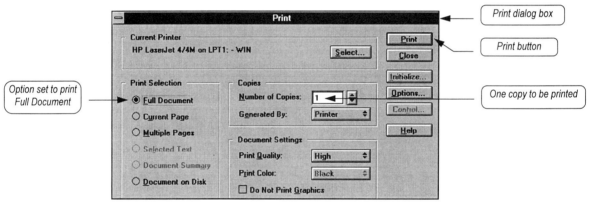

Figure 1 - 12

KEY TERMS

Backspace Key
Caps Lock Key
Close
Default Settings
Delete Key
Directory
Drive
Enter Key

Filename
Insert
Open
Save
Scroll
Shift Key
Typeover
Word wrap

INDEPENDENT PROJECTS

Independent Project 1.1: Notice to the Chefs

In this project you will use basic word processing tasks to create and print a notice to the Creative Cookery chefs about a Restaurant Show.

1. Click the **Open** button on the Power Bar to open a file named **notice.wpd**.

   *The **Open File** dialog box shows on screen so you can choose which file to open.*

2. Select the same drive and directory you used to save the file in Activity 1.2.

   *The list of filenames changes to reflect the active drive and directory. The filenames are always listed alphabetically. The **notice.wpd** file will be listed when the correct drive and directory is active.*

3. Click on the filename, **notice.wpd**.

   *In the **Open File** dialog box **notice.wpd** shows in the Filename text box.*

4. Click the **OK** button in the **Open File** dialog box.

   It takes a moment as WordPerfect brings the file on screen. The name of the file shows in the Title Bar.

5. Move the insertion point to the end of the file.

6. Press the **ENTER** key twice to start a new paragraph and leave a blank line.

7. Type: **If you would like to attend this event, call Ann Wilson at (516)555-4627. Creative Cookery will pay your show registration fee. Space is limited, so call soon to make your reservations.**

8. Press the **ENTER** key twice to start a new paragraph and leave a blank line.

9. Type: **If you want to notify any students about this event, contact Ann Wilson for brochures. Students are responsible to register and pay if they want to attend.**

10. Click the **Save** button on the Power Bar to save the file with the same name.

    *The title bar shows **unmodified** after the filename.*

11. To position the insertion point before **chefs** in the first line, click the mouse pointer before **chefs**.

    *The insertion point blinks before **chefs** in the first line. The mouse pointer can be moved to a different position and the insertion point still blinks before **chefs**.*

12. New text will be added at this position. If *Insert* shows on the status bar, continue to the next step. If *Typeover* shows on the status bar, press the **INSERT** key.

    ***Insert** shows on the status bar. New text can be typed at the position of the insertion point.*

13. Type: **Creative Cookery**

14. Position the insertion point before the comma in the first sentence by clicking the mouse pointer there.

15. Type: **and to further your knowledge in the culinary field**

16. Position the insertion point before **visit** in the first sentence.

17. Press the **DELETE** key as many times as needed to delete **visit and** and the space after **and**.

18. Position the insertion point after **George** in the third sentence.

19. Press the **BACKSPACE** key as many times as needed to delete **George** and the space before **George**.

20. Position the insertion point before **Area** in the last sentence of the first paragraph.

21. Press the **INSERT** key to activate *Typeover*.

    *The status bar shows **Typeover** as the active editing mode.*

22. Type: **City**

City replaces the word area.

23. Press the **INSERT** key to activate *Insert.*

    *The status bar shows **Insert** as the active editing mode.*

24. Does your document match the one shown in Figure 1-13?

25. Save the file with the same name by clicking on the **Save** button on the Power Bar.

    The file is stored on disk and unmodified shows after the filename in the Title Bar.

26. **Print** the file by clicking on the **Print** button on the Power Bar.

27. **Close** the file by double-clicking the **Control** menu box for the document window.

    *The screen clears and the title bar displays **[Document1 - unmodified].***

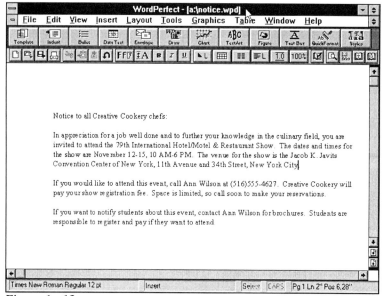

Figure 1 - 13

Independent Projects: 1.2: Mary's Reply Letter to Gregory

In this project you will complete a letter of reply from Mary to Gregory Zaleta. This project does not give you step-by-step instructions as in Independent Project 1.1. If you cannot remember how to complete a word processing task, refer to Table 1-2 or to where that task is presented previously in this lesson.

1. Open a file named **ltrzaleg.wpd**.

2. Move the insertion point to the end of the document.

3. Click on the **Date Text** button on the Button Bar to add today's date.

4. Press the **ENTER** key four times.

5. Type: **Mr. Gregory A. Zaleta**
         Creative Cookery
         Yaphank Commons
         Yaphank, NY 11980

6. Press the **ENTER** key twice.

7. Type: **Dear Mr. Zaleta**:

8. Press the **ENTER** key twice.

9. Type: **Thank you for the information about Creative Cookery. Before I register for classes, may I visit the school? I would like to have the opportunity to see the equipment in the kitchens and to meet some of the chefs and students.**

10. Press the **ENTER** key twice.

11. Type: **Please register me for the Open House this month referred to in your brochure. Thank you for your assistance.**

12. Press the **ENTER** key twice.

13. Type: **Sincerely,**

14. Press the **ENTER** key four times.

15. Type: **Mary Anderson**

Figure 1 - 14 shows the appearance of the screen at this point in the project.

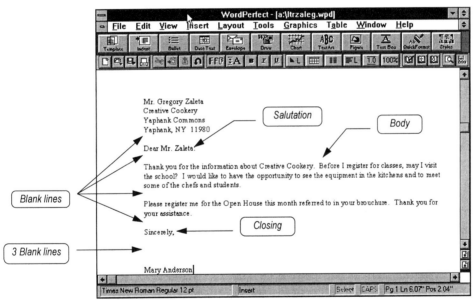

Figure 1 - 14

16. Proofread the file and make corrections as necessary.

17. **Save**, **print**, and **close** the file.

Independent Project 1.3: A Creative Cookery Course Description

In this project you will complete a Creative Cookery course description. This project does not give you step-by-step instructions as in Independent Project 1.1. If you cannot remember how to complete a word processing task, refer to Table 1-2 or to where that task is presented previously in this lesson.

1. Open a file named **cajun.wpd**.

2. Move the insertion point to the end of the document.

3. Type: **presents the wonderful secrets of New Orleans cuisine as well as legends and facts about this fascinating city. You will learn about the wide variety of seafood, fruit, and spices used in Cajun food. You will prepare Andouille Sausage Jambalaya with Tasso, Fried Eggplant Fingers with Mardi Gras Dip, Crayfish Etoufee, Banana Souffle, and Sweet-Potato Pecan Pie.**

4. Delete **wonderful** in the first sentence.

5. Delete **fruit,** in the second sentence.

6. Delete **Banana Souffle** in the third sentence.

7. Insert **at Creative Cookery** after **class** in the first sentence.

8. Insert **Shrimp Creole** before **Crayfish Etoufee** in the last sentence.

   After making these editing changes, the screen should appear as it does in Figure 1 - 15.

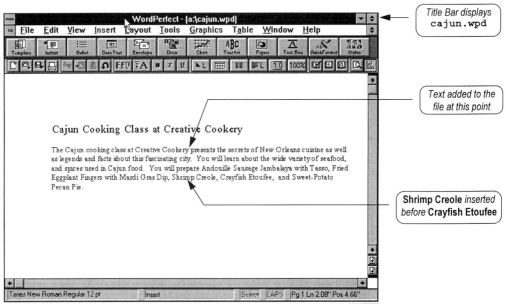

Figure 1 - 15

9. Proofread the document making any changes that are needed.

10. **Save**, **print**, and **close** the file.

Independent Project 1.4: A Letter from You to Creative Cookery

This project gives you an assignment that you create without steps to guide you. Create a letter from you to Creative Cookery that requests information about classes. Use your name and address as the return address. For the inside address use Creative Cookery, Yaphank Commons, Yaphank, NY 11980. Use full block letter style for the addresses, date, salutation, text, and closing (Full block style was used in the Lesson 1 Project). After you finish entering the text, make editing corrections. **Save**, **print**, and **close** the file.

Lesson 2 Editing a Document

Objectives

In this lesson you will learn how to:

- Open files
- Begin a new document
- Switch among open files
- Reveal codes
- Divide and combine paragraphs
- Undo and undelete

- Select text
- Move text
- Copy text
- Spell check a document
- Save a file with a new name
- Print multiple copies

PROJECT: EDITING A MEMO

In this project you will work with more *WordPerfect* features. You will create and edit a memo for the Creative Cookery school. A previously saved memo for Creative Cookery is stored with your data files. You will open this completed memo so that you can design the new memo in a similar manner.

As you proofread the new memo, you notice several editing changes that need to be made. One paragraph is too long and you decide to split it into two paragraphs. Another paragraph is too short and you decide to combine it with another. You continue to edit by deleting text, undoing typing, and undeleting text.

You decide to change the order of information in part of the file, so you move text. There is information that you want to show twice, so you copy it. There is information in the original memo that you want also in the new memo, so you copy information from the original memo to the memo you are editing. As the last editing task, you check the new memo for spelling errors.

You are not sure if the original version of the memo or the revised version is better for the Creative Cookery school. In order to get a second opinion, you decide not only to keep the original version of the memo as saved on disk, but also to save the revised version. To get opinions from two of your co-workers, you print two copies of the memo.

OPENING A FILE

Any *WordPerfect* document that has been saved as a file can be opened and used repeatedly. Several files can be open simultaneously, as each open file is placed in its own document window. You can switch from one document window to another document window to work in any open file.

When you click on the **Open** button on the Power Bar, *WordPerfect* displays the **Open File** dialog box, as in Figure 2 - 1. When you first open this dialog box, you will see that it is set to the default drive and directory for *WordPerfect for Windows* files, **c:\wpwin60**. If this drive and directory is where the file you want to open is stored, you will see its name listed alphabetically in the **Filename** listing. If the file to be opened is stored in a different drive and directory, select that drive and directory to access a list of filenames. When you see the **filename** you want to open in the list, you can click on it or type its name in the **Filename** text box. Once you see the correct filename in the Filename text box, clicking on **OK** will open the file into a document window.

When you click on the **Open** button on the Power Bar and *WordPerfect* displays the **Open File** dialog box, *.* is highlighted in the **Filename** text box. If you know the drive, directory, and name of the file to open, you may type it in. As you type the *.* disappears and your typing takes its place.

WordPerfect provides a shortcut technique for opening files that have been used recently. If you make the menu choice, **FILE,** a list of the four most recently used filenames shows at the bottom of that menu. If you click on a filename in that list, the file will open.

The limit to how many files can be open at the same time is nine. If you have nine open files and try to open another file, it will not be possible even though you are opening in the same manner you have always used. Whenever this happens, close a file that you are not using and then attempt to open the file.

If you are working with several files open as you attempt to open another, you may see this message: **This document is in use or is specified as read-only**. You may edit the document, but you must save it with a new name. In most cases **Continue**? means that the file you want to open is already open. Answer **No** to the message and switch to the file (Switch is an upcoming topic in this lesson).

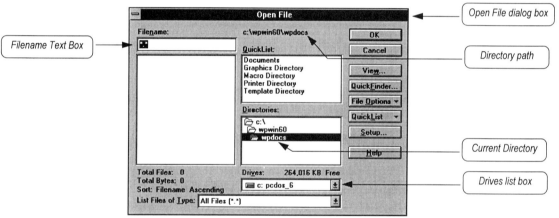

Figure 2 - 1

REMEMBER: Read the bulleted list that follows, but do not actually perform the steps until you reach Activity 2.1.

To open a file:

- Click the **Open** button on the Power Bar.

- If the file you want to open is not listed, change the drive and directory to indicate where the file is stored.

- Choose the file from the list of filenames by clicking it. Double-clicking the filename opens it immediately.

- Choose **OK**.

Activity 2.1: Opening a Memo File

Creative Cookery designs memos consistently. Before you create a new memo, you need to see the design, so you will open a previously saved memo file.

1. Click the **Open** button on the Power Bar.

    *The **Open File** dialog box shows listing filenames stored in the drive and directory named above QuickList.*

2. Choose the drive and directory where your data files are stored. Refer back to Lesson 1 if necessary.

    *The data files are listed in the **Open File** dialog box.*

3. Choose **memact21.wpd**.

    The filename is highlighted to be the active file among all the files listed. The filename indicates that it is a memo to be used for Activity 2.1

4. Choose the **OK** button.

    WordPerfect displays the file on screen in a document window. The Title bar displays the name of the file, as in Figure 2 - 2.

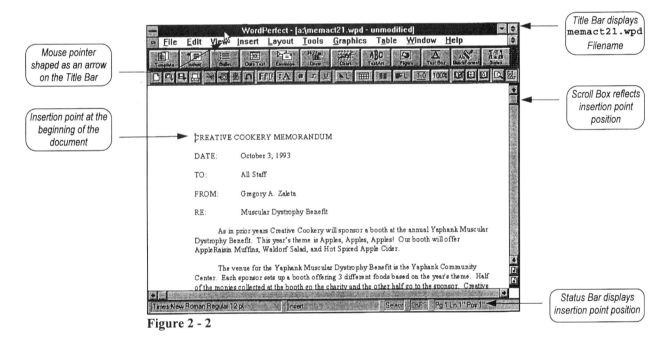

Figure 2 - 2

BEGINNING A NEW BLANK DOCUMENT

If you need a blank document window to begin a new file, use the **New Document** button on the Power Bar. Each new document is based on a *template* that sets formatting for the document. The Standard template is automatically assigned to a new document when you click the **New Document** button on the Power Bar. The Standard template is set with commonly used formatting: 8.5 by 11 inch paper, portrait orientation, 1 inch for all margins, single line spacing, left text alignment, tabs every half inch, and Times New Roman 12-point font.

To begin a new document:

- Click the **New Document** button [icon] on the Power Bar.

Activity 2.2: Begin a New Document

With the **memact21.wpd** file on screen, you want to begin work on a new memo.

1. Click the **New Document** button on the Power Bar.

   *The **memact21.wpd** disappears and a new blank document window appears. The Title Bar displays [Document2 - unmodified]. The Document number might vary depending on how many files are open. Even though you do not see the **memact21.wpd** file it is still open and available for use.*

2. Type: **CREATIVE COOKERY MEMORANDUM**

3. Press **ENTER** twice.

4. Type: **DATE:**

5. Press the **TAB** key.

6. Click the **Date Text** button on the button bar.

7. Press **ENTER** twice.

8. Type the rest of the memo as shown in Figure 2 - 3   Memo, First Draft. Use the **TAB** key to position text to align with the date. You may notice some typing errors. Don't correct them yet. You will use Speller in another activity. Remember that your lines may end at different places than as shown in the figure.

9. **Save** the document using the filename, **memact22.wpd**.

TO: All Staff

FROM: Gregory A. Zaleta

RE: Muscular Distrophy Benefit

    As in prior years Creative Cookery will sponsor a booth at the annual Yaphank Muscular Dystrophy Benefit. This year's theme is Chocolate, Chocolate, Chocolate! Our booth will offer White Chocolate Chip Macadamia Nut Cookies, Strawberries Dipped in in Milk Chocolate, and Iced Mocha Cappuccino. The working schedule assignments are as follows:

Group A: Friday, November 4
Group C: Sunday, November 6
Group B: Saturday, November 5

    In the past years our participation in this benefit not only helped the community but also benefited Creative Cookery financially and by getting our name out in the public.
    The financial gains are placed in our New Equipment fund. Word of mouth recomendations always speak louder than mass mailings.
    Thank you for making this a success for us in the past. We look forward too another successful event this year.

Figure 2 - 3 Memo, First Draft

SWITCHING BETWEEN OPEN FILES

In *WordPerfect for Windows* you can work with several documents simultaneously. Each document is in a document window. One reason you might wish to work with several open windows is to make copying or moving text between documents easy.

If you have a document open and you open another document or start a new document, the new document window hides the previous document window. To work with one of the open windows, you switch to it. Choosing **WINDOW** in the menu displays the names of all currently open files. When you click on a filename in the **Window** menu, the document window for that file becomes the active window and is displayed on the screen.

To switch between open files:

- From the Menu Bar choose **WINDOW**.

- A list of each open file shows (Figure 2 - 4).

- Click on the filename you want to display.

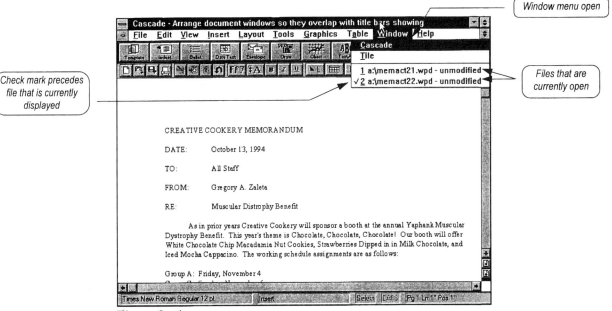

Figure 2 - 4

Activity 2.3: Switching between the New and Old Memos

1. Choose **WINDOW**.

2. Choose the filename, **memact21.wpd**.

   The 1993 memo document window is displayed. The new memo document window is active but not displayed.

3. Choose **WINDOW** again.

4. Choose the new file, **memact22.wpd**.

   Now the new memo document window is displayed and the 1993 memo document window is active but not displayed.

REVEALING CODES

When you use *WordPerfect's* Reveal Codes, the formatting codes for your document are displayed along with the text. A *code* stores information that determines how the document will look when it is printed. Some codes are inserted in your document when you press the **ENTER** key, the **TAB** key, or use a *WordPerfect* feature. Other codes are placed in your document automatically by *WordPerfect*, such as a word wrap code at the end of some lines to make the text return to the left side and move down one line.

Revealing codes is useful to gain insight about your document. Another reason to reveal codes is for making editing changes to a document. Codes can be modified or deleted. You can type, edit, and do all your normal *WordPerfect* work while the Reveal Codes feature is visible.

Reveal Codes splits the document window into two sections: the regular *WordPerfect* document area at the top of the window and the Reveal Codes area at the bottom of the window. The Reveal Codes area shows the same text you see in the regular window at the insertion point. In Reveal Codes the insertion point appears as a red box, spaces appear as diamonds, and codes as buttons. The most common codes in every document are [SRt] for soft return, [HRt] for hard return, and [Left Tab]. *Soft Return* indicates where word wrap occurs and *Hard Return* indicates where you have pressed the **ENTER** key.

When you are finished working with the codes, they can be hidden so that only the document window with text is shown.

To reveal codes:

- Choose **VIEW/Reveal Codes**.

To hide reveal codes:

- Choose **VIEW/Reveal Codes**.

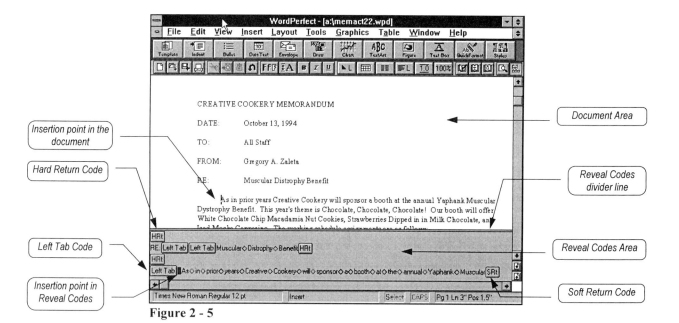

Figure 2 - 5

Activity 2.4: Revealing Codes

First you will reveal codes in the memo document to become familiar with how the codes display. In an upcoming activity you will see how codes affect paragraphs.

1. Choose **VIEW/Reveal Codes.**

   At the bottom of the screen is the Reveal Codes area. It shows codes along with the document text. The red box in the Reveal Codes area shows where the insertion point is active.

2. Press any arrow key and note the change in position of the red box (insertion point) in the Reveal Codes area of the screen.

3. Find where the most common codes, [HRt], [SRt], and [Left Tab] show for the memo.

   *[HRt] shows where the **ENTER** key was pressed. [SRt] indicates where word wrap moved the text down to the next line. [Left Tab], shows where the **TAB** key was pressed.*

4. Choose **VIEW/Reveal Codes.**

   Reveal Codes is hidden.

DIVIDING AND COMBINING PARAGRAPHS

If the editing change you want to make is to divide a long paragraph into two paragraphs or combine two short paragraphs into one longer paragraph, you will find it is quite easy to do.

The first step for dividing a long paragraph into two paragraphs is to position the insertion point where you want to make the split (where the second paragraph will begin). Since *WordPerfect* automatically inserts, you can press the keys you normally use to begin a paragraph, the **ENTER** key followed by the **TAB** key and the paragraph becomes two paragraphs.

The first step for combining two paragraphs into one is to position the insertion point at the end of the first paragraph. Then by pressing the **DELETE** key twice, the **ENTER** and the **TAB** that divided the two paragraphs are removed and you have combined the paragraphs into one paragraph.

To divide a paragraph into two paragraphs:

* Move the insertion point at the beginning of the sentence where the second paragraph will begin.
* Press the **ENTER** key.
* Press the **TAB** key.

To combine two paragraphs:

* Move the insertion point at the end of the first paragraph.
* Press the **DELETE** key twice.

Activity 2.5: Dividing and Combining Paragraphs

In this activity you will work with Reveal Codes displayed to see the change in codes to a document as you divide and combine paragraphs.

1. Choose **VIEW/Reveal Codes** to see the Reveal Codes area at the bottom of the screen**.**

2. Move the insertion point to the beginning of the sentence, **The working schedule assignments are as...**

3. Press **ENTER.**

The sentence splits from the first paragraph and moves down to the beginning of the next line. The [HRt] code is inserted into the document.

4. Press **TAB**.

The new paragraph is indented and a [Left Tab] code shows before the paragraph text, as shown in Figure 2 - 6.

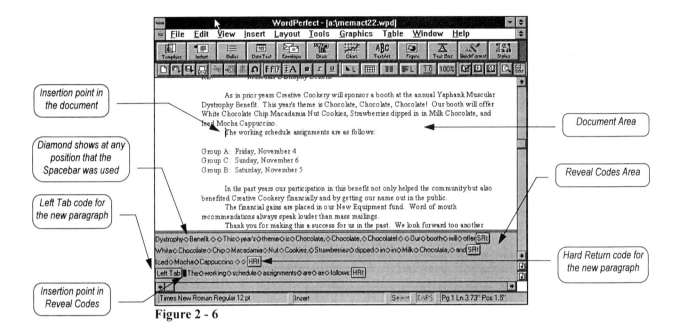

Figure 2 - 6

5. Move the insertion point to the end of the sentence that ends, **...by getting our name out to the public.**

6. Press the **DELETE** key twice.

The [HRt] and [Left Tab] codes are removed and that sentence combines with the next paragraph into one paragraph.

7. Press the **SPACEBAR** twice.

8. Choose **VIEW/Reveal Codes** to hide the codes.

SELECTING TEXT

Before you can modify text, you must select the amount of text to modify. Text can be selected with the mouse, by making menu choices, or by using key combinations. Any amount of text can be selected: one letter, one word, several words, a sentence, a paragraph, a page, or the entire document. Selected text appears highlighted on the screen.

There are many ways to modify selected text. Deleting, moving, and copying selected text are only a few of the many possibilities; however, only one selection can be modified at a time. It is not possible to select one paragraph, several words, and a sentence to delete all at one time. You must select the paragraph and delete it. Then select the words and delete them. At that point you can select the sentence to delete. Table 2-1 lists the techniques for selecting text easily with the mouse.

Table 2 - 1: Selecting Text with the Mouse

Selection	Mouse Technique
Word	Double-click on the word.
Sentence	Triple-click anywhere on the sentence.
Paragraph	Quadruple-click anywhere on the paragraph or double-click in the left margin.
A group of text	Drag the mouse pointer across the text or click at the beginning of the selection and **SHIFT+click** at the end.

Some text selections are accomplished more readily by making menu choices rather than using the mouse. Table 2-2 details the menu choices for selecting text.

Table 2 - 2: Selecting with the Menu

Selection	Menu Choice
Sentence	**EDIT/Select, Sentence**
Paragraph	**EDIT/Select, Paragraph**
Page	**EDIT/Select, Page**
Entire document	**EDIT/Select, All**

Selected text →

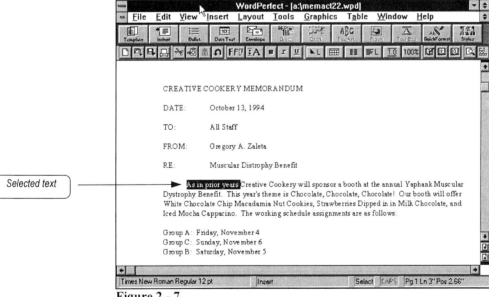

Figure 2 - 7

Once the text you want to work with is selected, and you see the highlighting on the screen, then you can modify the selection. If you realize that you do not want to work with the selection, you can deselect with the mouse by clicking in the document area or with the keyboard by pressing an arrow key.

Selected text can be replaced by typing. Sometimes this is useful as an editing technique. For example, if your document shows the name, George Anderson, and it needs to be changed to show Mary Robinson, select George Anderson and type Mary Robinson. You will see that Mary Robinson replaced George Anderson. It is important to deselect when you are finished with modifications.

CAUTION: *It is important to deselect your text before you continue to type to avoid losing text accidentally. However, to recover text accidentally lost, click on the **Undo** button on the Power Bar or select **EDIT/Undo typing**. For further information see section on Undo and Undelete.*

To deselect text:

• Click the mouse pointer anywhere outside the selection.

DELETING SELECTED TEXT

One way to delete selected text is to press the **DELETE** key. Another way to delete selected text is to click on the **Cut** button on the Power Bar.

To delete text:

• Select the text.

• Press the **DELETE** key.

USING UNDO AND UNDELETE

If you make a mistake as you are working in *WordPerfect*, Undo will reverse your last editing action. If you delete text that you want to bring back into the document, Undelete restores deleted text. Unlike Undo, which lets you restore information in its original location, Undelete lets you restore deleted text at the insertion point. Another difference between Undo and Undelete is that Undo works only with your last editing action, while Undelete stores the three previous deletions. If you use the **Cut** button on the Power Bar to delete text, you must use the **Paste** button or Undo to restore the information.

To undo a mistake:

• Click the **Undo** button on the Power Bar.

To undelete text:

• Move the insertion point to the position for restoring the text.

• Choose **EDIT/Undelete**.

• Choose **Previous** or **Next** buttons until the text you want to restore is displayed.

• Choose **Restore**.

Activity 2.6: Deleting Text, Undoing a Mistake, and Undeleting Text

In this activity you will delete selected text. Then you will select text and accidentally type from the keyboard. As the selected text disappears and the new information is entered, you will use Undo to correct the mistake. Lastly, you decide to restore the text you deleted first by using Undelete to bring it back.

1. Try using the different techniques for selecting text as shown in Tables 2-1 and 2-2.

2. Drag the mouse across the phrase, **As in prior years,** in the first paragraph.

   The selected text is highlighted. The status bar displays Select in black to indicate there is an active selection in the file.

3. Press the **DELETE** key.

    The selected text disappears. The remaining text adjusts. The status bar shows Select in gray to indicate there is no active selection in the file.

4. Triple-click the last sentence to select it.

    The selected sentence is highlighted. The status bar shows Select in black to indicate there is an active selection in the file.

5. You will purposely make a mistake by typing: **Don't be**

    The text that you just typed replaced the selection as shown in Figure 2 - 8. You did not want to lose that sentence.

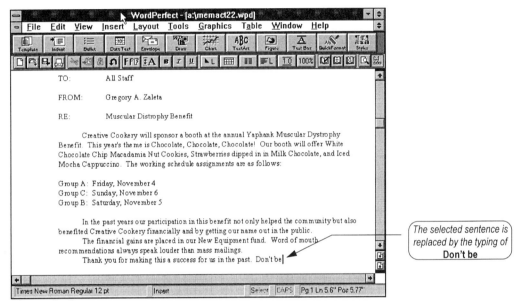

Figure 2 - 8

6. Click on the **Undo** button on the Power Bar.

    *Your last action, replacing the sentence with **Don't be**, is reversed. **Don't be** is deleted and the sentence is restored.*

7. Now you realize that you want to bring the text that you deleted from the first paragraph back into the document. Move the insertion point to the beginning of the first paragraph.

8. Choose **EDIT/Undelete**.

    The Undelete dialog box and the last deletion appears, selected at the position of the insertion point.

9. Click on the **Previous** button.

    The previous deletion shows, selected at the position of the insertion point.

10. Click on the **Restore** button.

    The text is restored to the document at the insertion point location.

MOVING TEXT

A common editing task is moving text to a different location in the document. With *WordPerfect* you can move text using cut and paste, or drag and drop. Cut and paste is better for anyone unaccustomed to using the mouse. Once you have plenty of mouse experience, you might prefer using drag and drop.

To move text:

- Select the text to be moved.
- Choose **EDIT/Cut** or click on the **Cut** button 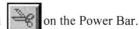 on the Power Bar.
- Move the insertion point to the new location.
- Choose **EDIT/Paste** or click on the **Paste** button  on the Power Bar.

COPYING TEXT

The technique used for copying text varies slightly from moving text. As with moving, you have two alternative methods for copying text: copy and paste, or drag and drop.

To copy text:

- Select the text to be copied.
- Click on the **Copy** button on the Power Bar or choose **EDIT/Copy**.
- Move the insertion point to the new location.
- Click on the **Paste** button on the Power Bar or choose **EDIT/Paste**.

Activity 2.7: Moving and Copying Text

In this activity you will move text to correct the order of the days for the working schedule assignments. To catch the reader's attention, you will copy the first line of the text so that it also shows at the end of the document.

1. Drag across **Group B: Saturday, November 5** to select the text to be moved.

   The text and the space to the end of the line are highlighted.

2. Click on the **Cut** button on the Power Bar.

   The selected text disappears from the screen. The computer is storing the information in the Clipboard.

3. Move the insertion point to before **Group C**.

4. Click on the **Paste** button on the Power Bar.

   The text appears in the new location.

5. Select the first line of text, **CREATIVE COOKERY MEMORANDUM**.

   The selected text is highlighted.

6. Click on the **Copy** button on the Power Bar.

   The selected text stays on the screen. The computer removed the previous information from the Clipboard and is now storing the copied information.

7. Move the insertion point to the end of the file.

8. Press the **ENTER** key twice.

9. Click on the **Paste** button on the Power Bar.

   The text appears in its original location and also at the end of the file, as shown in Figure 2 - 9 .

Figure 2 - 9

COPYING OR MOVING TEXT FROM ONE FILE TO ANOTHER FILE

One of the major advantages when working with a Windows application is the ability to copy or move text from one file to another file. There is only one step to add to the technique used when working with only one file. When you copy or move from one file to another, you will use the **WINDOW** menu to switch to the other file in order to position the insertion point.

To copy text from one file to another file:

- Select the text to be copied.
- Click on the **Copy** button on the Power Bar.
- Choose **WINDOW** and click on the name of the file to receive the information.
- Move the insertion point to the new location.
- Click on the **Paste** button on the Power Bar.

To move text from one file to another file:

- Select the text to be moved.
- Click on the **Cut** button on the Power Bar.
- Choose **WINDOW** and click on the name of the file to receive the information.
- Move the insertion point to the new location.
- Click on the **Paste** button on the Power Bar.

Activity 2.8: Copying Text from One Memo to Another Memo File

In this activity you copy a paragraph from the 1993 memo into the new memo.

1. Choose **WINDOW**.

    *At the bottom of the **Window** menu, a list of all the open files shows.*

2. To switch to the 1993 memo, click on **memact21.wpd**.

    The document window displays the 1993 memo.

3. With the mouse pointer to the left of the second paragraph, double-click to select the paragraph.

    The second paragraph is highlighted, as in Figure 2 - 10.

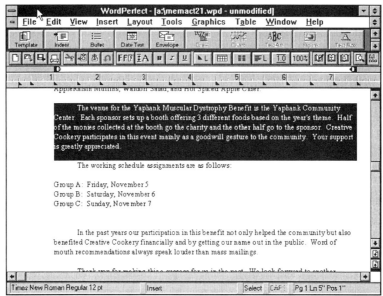

Figure 2 - 10

4. Click on the **Copy** button on the Power Bar.

    The selected text stays on the screen. The computer removes the previous information from the Clipboard and stores the newly copied information.

5. Choose **WINDOW**.

6. Click on **memact22.wpd**.

7. *The document window displays the new memo.*

8. Move the insertion point to the beginning of the second paragraph.

9. Click on the **Paste** button on the Power Bar.

    The paragraph from the 1993 memo is the second paragraph in the new memo.

    See Figure 2 - 11. WordPerfect adjusts the text for the new paragraph.

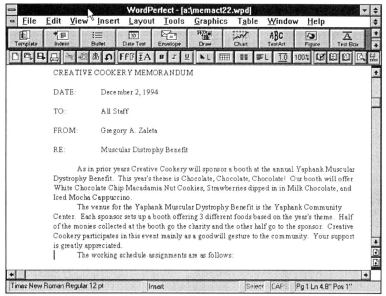

Figure 2 - 11

USING SPELLER

WordPerfect will check for spelling errors in a document. Common editing procedure includes using the Speller before printing. The Speller will identify misspelled words, duplicate words, and irregular capitalization. *WordPerfect* will stop at any word not included in its dictionary.

When the Speller stops at a misspelled word, you can choose a replacement word from a list of correctly spelled suggestions. The selected replacement will take the place of the misspelled word and then continue to the next misspelling.

The Speller cannot be a substitute for proofreading. If there are any words that are incorrect but not misspelled, Speller will not highlight them. For example, if your file contains **Welcome too our office**, *WordPerfect* will not stop at **too** as a misspelled word.

To use the Speller:

- Click on the **Speller** button ![button] on the Power Bar.

- The **Speller** dialog box opens (Figure 2 - 12).

- Choose the **Start** button.

- Choose one of the options described in Table 2-3.

Table 2 - 3: Speller Options

Option	What It Does
Replace	Replaces the word with the text specified in the **Replace With** text box. You can select one of the words in the **Suggestions** list box or edit the word in the text box.
Resume	Continues a spell check that is paused for editing.
Skip Once	Skips one occurrence of the word.
Skip Always	Skips every occurrence of the word.
Add	Adds the word to the dictionary.
Suggest	Displays additional words in the **Suggestions** list box.

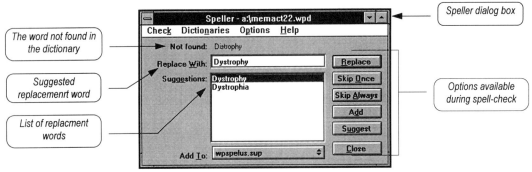

The word not found in the dictionary

Suggested replacemenrt word

List of replacment words

Speller dialog box

Options available during spell-check

Figure 2 - 12

Activity 2.9: Spell Checking the Memo

Before you print the edited memo, you will check for spelling errors.

1. Click on the **Speller** button on the Power Bar.

    *The **Speller** dialog box appears.*

2. Click on the **Start** button.

3. The first word that does not match any words in the dictionary is highlighted. Suggestions are listed for possible replacement.

    *Figure 2 - 13 shows **Zaleta** highlighted by Speller.*

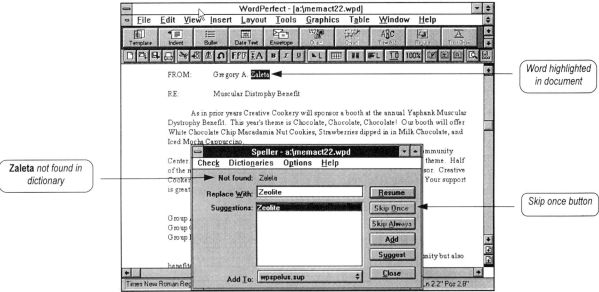

Zaleta not found in dictionary

Word highlighted in document

Skip once button

Figure 2 - 13

4. Since the word is a correctly spelled proper noun, click on the **Skip Once** button.

    The next word that might be misspelled is highlighted. Suggestions are listed for possible replacement.

5. Click on the correctly spelled, **Dystrophy**.

    *The correct spelling shows in the **Replace With** text box.*

6. Click on the **Replace** button.

*WordPerfect makes the change in the document so that **Dystrophy** is now spelled correctly.*

7. Click on the **Skip Always** button when Speller stops at **Yaphank**.

    *WordPerfect moves on to the next word. The **Skip Always** choice makes WordPerfect bypass Yaphank if it appears again.*

8. To remove one of the duplicate words, click on the **Replace** button (Figure 2 - 14).

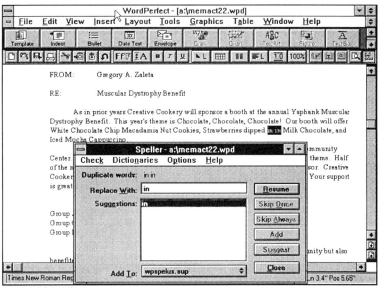

Figure 2 - 14

10. Click on the **Skip Once** button at **cappuccino**.

11. Click on the **Replace** button to place the correctly spelled **recommendations** in the document.

12. When asked "**Spell-check completed. Close Speller?**", click on **Yes** (Figure 2 - 15).

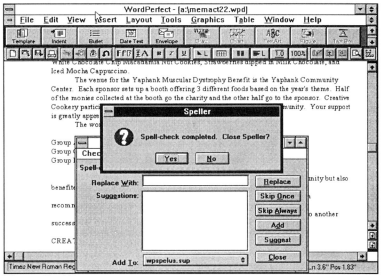

Figure 2 - 15

13. Note that Speller did not stop at **too** in the last sentence. Always proofread a document in addition to using the Speller.

SAVING A FILE WITH A NEW NAME

After editing a file, you may decide that you want to keep the original version of the file and also save the modified version. Since two different versions of a file cannot have the same name, you cannot save the modified version by clicking on the **Save** button on the Power Bar. The **Save** button saves the modified file with the same name by replacing the original version of the file. To save the modified file with a new name, you will choose **Save As** from the **FILE** menu.

To save a file with a new name:

- Choose **FILE/Save As**.

- Type the new name in the **Filename** text box.

- Click on the **OK** button.

Activity 2.10: Saving the Memo with a New Name

In this activity you will keep the original version of the memo with the name **memact22.wpd** and save the modified version of the memo with a new name.

1. Choose **FILE/Save As**.

   *The **Save As** dialog box appears.*

2. Type in the new filename: **memnew**

   *Figure 2 - 16 shows the **Save As** dialog box with the new filename entered.*

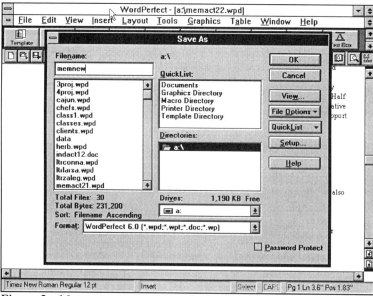

Figure 2 - 16

3. Click on the **OK** button.

   *The filename appears on the title bar as [**memnew.wpd - unmodified**].*

4. Open the **memact22.wpd** file.

   *This document, **memact22.wpd**, is the original version of the memo.*

5. Choose **WINDOW**.

   The names of all the open files show at the bottom of the Window menu.

6. Click on **memnew.wpd**.

   *This document, **memnew.wpd**, is the modified version of the memo.*

PRINTING MULTIPLE COPIES

You can print more than one copy of a document. The **Print** dialog box includes a text box for **Number of Copies**.

To print multiple copies:

- Click on the **Print** button 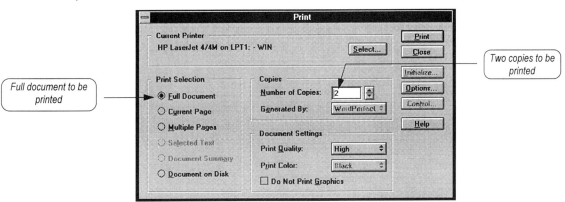 on the Power Bar.
- Click in the **Number of Copies** text box.
- Delete the current number and type in the number of copies to print.
- Click on the **Print** button.

Activity 2.11: Printing Two Copies of the Memo

In this activity you will print two copies of the memo by using the **Print** dialog box.

1. Click on the **Print** button of the Power Bar.

   *The **Print** dialog box appears.*

2. Click in the **Number of Copies** text box.

   *The insertion point appears in the **Number of Copies** text box.*

3. Depending on the position of the insertion point, use either the **BACKSPACE** or **DELETE** key to remove the number.

4. Type: **2.**

   The Print dialog box shows as in Figure 2 - 17.

Figure 2 - 17

5. Click on the **Print** button.

   WordPerfect takes a moment to set up the print job, then prints two copies of the memo.

KEY TERMS

Code	Soft Return
Copy and Paste	Speller
Cut and Paste	Standard Template
Hard Return	Switch
New Document	Tab
Reveal Codes	Undelete
Save As	Undo
Selecting	

INDEPENDENT PROJECTS

Independent Project 2.1: Moving Text

In this project you will open a file containing the class schedule for one day at Creative Cookery. The class times in the file are not in the correct order. You will use *WordPerfect's* move feature to place the class information in the correct time sequence.

1. Open the file named **schedule.wpd**.

2. Use **move** to reorder the classes into the correct time sequence. For each move, always begin by selecting the text to be moved. Refer to Table 2-1 for ways to select text. Then use either the Power Bar or the appropriate Menu commands. Table 2-4 reviews the various move techniques. Figure 2 - 18 Final Version of the Schedule Document shows the final version of the schedule.

3. Spell check the document using the **Speller** button on the Power Bar,.

4. **Save** the file with the same name.

5. **Print** two copies of the document.

6. **Close** the file.

Creative Cookery Class Schedule
November 21, 1994

9:00 AM	Basic Sauces	Room 111
10:00 AM	Knife Selection and Use	Room 222
11:00 AM	Jams and Jellies	Room 111
1:00 PM	Chocolate	Room 222
2:00 PM	Advanced Sauces	Room 111
3:00 PM	Vegetables for Garnish	Room 222
4:00 PM	Presentation Techniques	Room 123

Figure 2 - 18 Final Version of the Schedule Document

Independent Project 2.2: Copying Text

In this project you will use a file that lists Creative Cookery's classes and identifies the chef who teaches the class. Some of the classes do not show a chef's name. You will use the copy feature in *WordPerfect* to complete the document.

1. Open the file named **chef.wpd**.

2. Use *WordPerfect's* copy feature to duplicate the chefs' names as shown in Figure 2 - 19 Final Version of the Chefs Document. For each copy always begin by selecting the text to be copied. Refer to Table 2-1 for ways to select text. Then use either the Power Bar or the appropriate Menu commands. Table 2-4 reviews the various copy techniques.

3. **Save** and **close** the file.

```
Chefs for the Creative Cookery Classes


Basic Sauces
Thomas McFarland

Advanced Sauces
Thomas McFarland

Cajun Cooking
Paul Johnson

Chocolate
Thomas McFarland

Herbs and Spices
Paul Johnson

International Cuisine
Mimi Rogers

Jams and Jellies
Mimi Rogers

Knife Selection and Use
Joyce Jones

Presentation Techniques
Joyce Jones

Vegetables for Garnish
Joyce Jones
```

Figure 2 - 19 Final Version of the Chefs Document

Independent Project 2.3: Copying From One File To Another File

In this project you will work with two letters. You will copy two paragraphs from one letter to the other letter. You will switch from one file to the other to accomplish this task.

1. Open the files named **ltrlarsa.wpd** and **ltrconna.wpd**.

2. Copy the last two paragraphs from the letter to Andrew Larson to become the last two paragraphs in the letter to Allison Conner.

3. Begin the copy by selecting the text to copy. Refer to Table 2-1 for ways to select.

    Figure 2 - 20 shows the document with selected paragraphs.

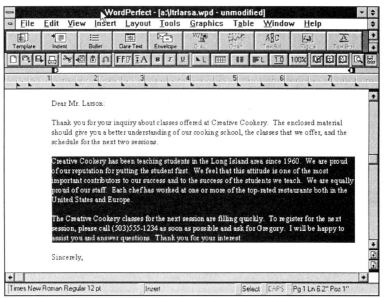

Figure 2 - 20

4. Choose to copy the text using one of the methods shown in Table 2-4.

5. Use the **WINDOW** menu command for switching to the letter to Allison Conner.

6. Position the insertion point correctly, then paste the two paragraphs.

    *Figure 2 - 21 shows the result of the **paste** command.*

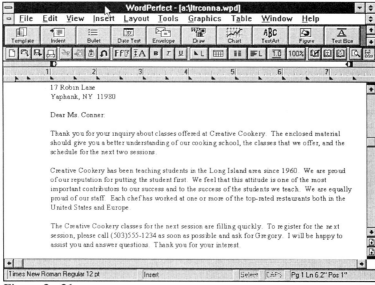

Figure 2 - 21

7. Save the files with the same names.

Independent Project 2.4: Starting A New Document

In this project begin a new document and type paragraph about the *WordPerfect* features you have learned to use. Proofread the document and make any appropriate editing changes such as inserting, deleting, or moving text. Use the Speller to check for misspelled words. Save the document with the name **mywdprft.wpd**.

Lesson 3 Enhancing Documents

Objectives:

In this lesson you will learn how to:

- Change text alignment

- Emphasize text with bold, underline, and italics

- Use fonts to change the style and size of text

- Create a bullet list

- Add a special character to a document

PROJECT: A COOKING CLASS ANNOUNCEMENT

Creative Cookery is about to launch its next series of cooking classes and needs an attractive, eye-catching announcement that can be mailed to prospective students. In this project, you will open and edit a cooking class announcement so that it looks like the one shown in Figure 3 - 1.

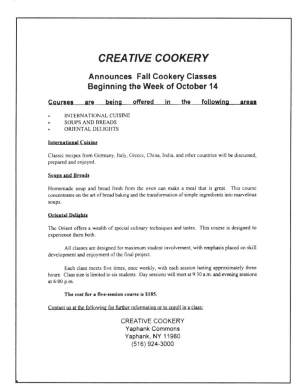

Figure 3 - 1

ALIGNING TEXT

You can align text in five ways: left justified, right justified, center justified, full justified, and all justified. *Left justified* means that the text is even at the left margin and ragged at the right margin. *Right justified* means that text is even at the right margin and ragged at the left margin. *Center justified* means that text is centered between the left and right margins. *Full justified* means that the text is even at both the left and right margins except for the last line of a paragraph. *All justified* means that text is even at both the left and right margins, including the last line of a paragraph. The default is left justified. See Figure 3 - 2 for examples of text alignment.

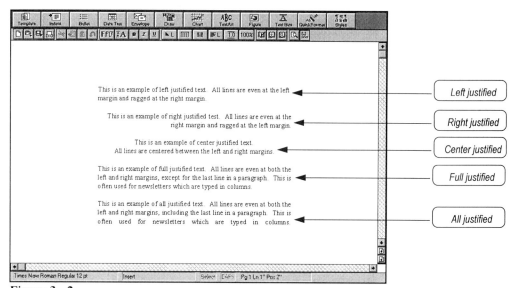

Figure 3 - 2

To change text alignment:

- Place the insertion point where the alignment change is to occur.
- Click on the **Justification** button on the Power Bar.
- Drag down to select **Right**, **Center**, **Full**, or **All**.

To change the alignment of a section of text:

- Place the insertion point where the alignment change is to occur.
- Select the text.
- Click on the **Justification** button on the Power Bar.
- Drag down to select **Right**, **Center**, **Full**, or **All**.

Activity 3.1 - Aligning Text

In the first part of this activity, you will change the alignment for sections of your text. First, you will center the title lines at the top of the document. Next, you will center the name and address lines at the bottom of the document. You will then use all justification to spread center a line between the left and right margins.

1. Open the **class1.wpd** document.
2. Place the insertion point in front of the first title line, **CREATIVE COOKERY**.

3. Click the left mouse button and drag the I-beam down to select the three title lines as in Figure 3 - 3.

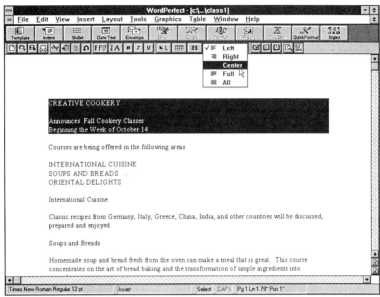

Figure 3 - 3

4. Use the **Justification** button on the Power Bar to center the selected text by clicking on the button and dragging down to Center.

To access the information on some of the Power Bar buttons and in some dialog boxes click on the button with the left mouse button, keep the mouse button depressed, and then drag up or down to select an option. The option is selected when the mouse button is released.

5. Click outside the selected text to remove the highlighting.

The title lines should be centered between the left and right margins. See Figure 3 - 4

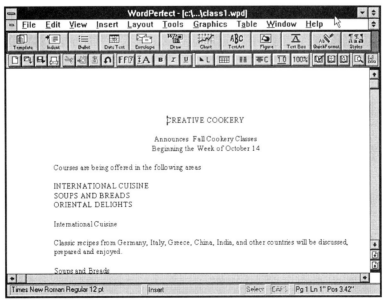

Figure 3 - 4

6. Place the insertion point in front of the name and address.

7. Select the four lines. See Figure 3 - 5.

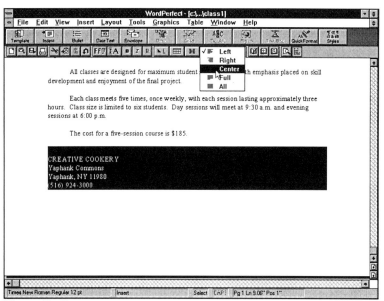

Figure 3 - 5

8. Use the **Justification** button on the Power Bar to center the lines.

9. Remove the highlighting.

Figure 3 - 6 shows the name and address centered between the left and right margins. If you wanted to change to a different alignment, you would select the text again, click on the **Justification** *button on the Power Bar, and choose a different alignment.*

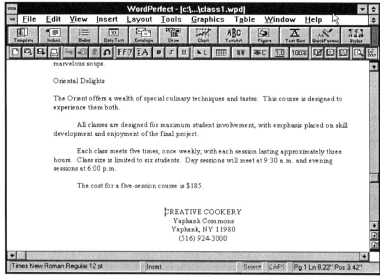

Figure 3 - 6

As you have worked with WordPerfect, you have found that alternative methods are provided to accomplish the same task. In this and later activities, you will have an opportunity to use different methods to accomplish various tasks. For example, you may use menus, keyboard commands, the Button Bar, or the Power Bar. You will spread a line between the left and right margins using the Layout menu. The Layout menu contains formatting commands.

10. Place the insertion point in front of the line beginning, **Courses are being offered**... at the top of the document.

11. Select the line. See Figure 3 - 7.

Figure 3 - 7

12. Click on **LAYOUT** in the Menu Bar.

13. Click on **Justification**.

The menus shown in Figure 3 - 8 appear.

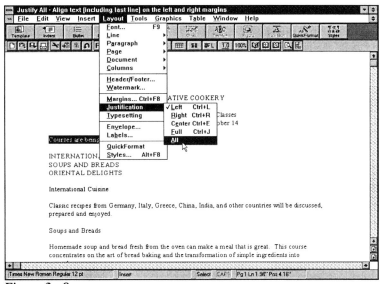

Figure 3 - 8

14. Click on **All**.

15. Remove the highlighting.

    Figure 3 - 9 shows the line spread between the left and right margins.

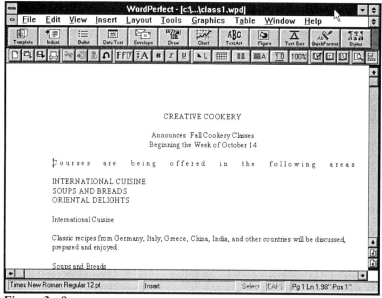

Figure 3 - 9

You will now change the alignment for the remaining text in the document to full justification without first selecting the text.

16. Place the insertion point at the beginning of the paragraph beginning **Classic Recipes from Germany**... See Figure 3 - 10.

Figure 3 - 10

17. Choose **LAYOUT/Justification,Full**

    When you make changes to a document's appearance or format, hidden codes are embedded in the text. All text following the code will be affected by the code unless another code of the same type is encountered.

18. Choose **VIEW/Reveal Codes**.

    You have embedded a Full Justification code in the text. This code affects your document until the end of the document or another format code is encountered, in this case, the Center justification code in front of the address. Figure 3 - 11 shows the Full justification code.

19. Locate the Full Justfication code. Place the insertion point in front of the code to display the code contents.

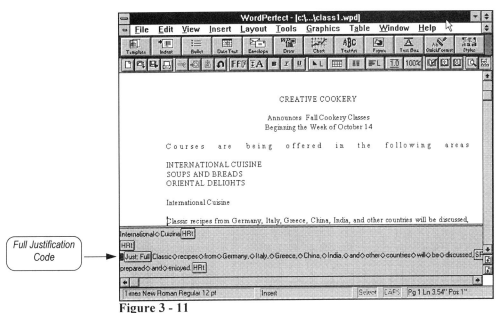

Figure 3 - 11

20. Scroll down and locate the Center Justification code.

21. Place the insertion point in front of the code to display the code contents.

22. Choose **VIEW/Reveal Codes** to recombine the screen.

    You will now continue to add other enhancements to the class announcement.

CHANGING THE APPEARANCE OF TEXT

The appearance of text can be changed in various ways. The most common way is to emphasize the text with bold, underline, or italics. You can add text emphasis to existing text, or you can add emphasis to text as you type it.

To change the appearance of existing text:

- Select the text.

- Click on the **Bold**, **Italics**, or **Underline** button on the Power Bar.

KEYBOARD ALTERNATIVE:

- Select the text.
- Press the **CTRL + B** keys for bold.
- Press the **CTRL + I** keys for italics.
- Press the **CTRL + U** keys for underline.

To change the appearance of text as you type it:

- Click on the **Bold**, **Italics**, or **Underline** button on the Power Bar to start the text emphasis.
- Type the text.
- Click on the **Bold**, **Italics**, or **Underline** button on the Power Bar to end the text emphasis.

Activity 3.2: Changing Text Appearance

In this activity you will add bold and underlining to the three paragraph heading lines, using the Power Bar buttons.

1. Place the insertion point in front of the cooking class heading line, **International Cuisine**

2. Select the line. See Figure 3 - 12

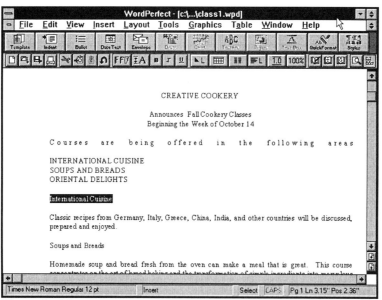

Figure 3 - 12

3. Click on the **Bold** button on the Power Bar.

4. With **International Cuisine** still selected, click on the **Underline** button on the Power Bar.

5. With **International Cuisine** still selected, click on the **Italics** button on the Power Bar.

6. Remove the highlighting.

Figure 3 - 13

Figure 3 - 13 shows the line darker than the rest of your text, underlined, and in italics.

You can remove text emphasis in several ways. One way is to reselect the text and click on the appropriate Power Bar button.

7. Select **International Cuisine** again.

8. Click on the **Italics** button to remove the italics.

9. Remove the highlighting.

The line is no longer in italics.

10. Add bold and underlining to the cooking class heading lines, **Soups and Breads** and **Oriental Delights**. See Figure 3 - 14.

Figure 3 - 14

Whenever you add bold, underline, or italics to your text, hidden codes are embedded in your document. Another way to remove text emphasis is to delete the hidden code. In the next part of this activity, you will insert and then remove an appearance code.

11. Place your insertion point in front of the line beginning, **The cost for a five-session...**

12. Select the line. See Figure 3 - 15.

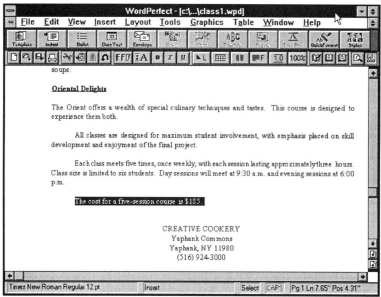

Figure 3 - 15

13. Click on the **Bold** button on the Power Bar.

14. Remove the highlighting.

15. Choose **VIEW/Reveal Codes**

16. Locate the Bold codes that appear at the beginning and the end of the line. See Figure 3 - 16.

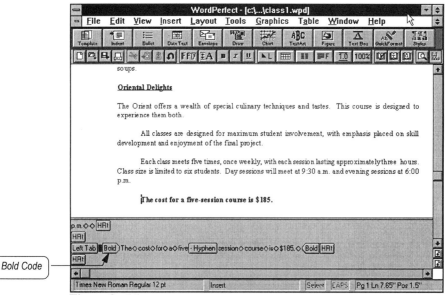

Figure 3 - 16

17. Delete one of the codes by placing the insertion point in front of the code and pressing the **DELETE** key.

18. Recombine your screen.

    By deleting one of the Bold codes, the bold emphasis is removed from the line of text. Underlining and italics can be removed in the same way.

    Up to this point, you have added text emphasis to existing text by selecting it. Now you will add text emphasis to text as you type it.

19. Place your insertion point on the blank line above the name and address at the bottom of the announcement. See Figure 3 - 17.

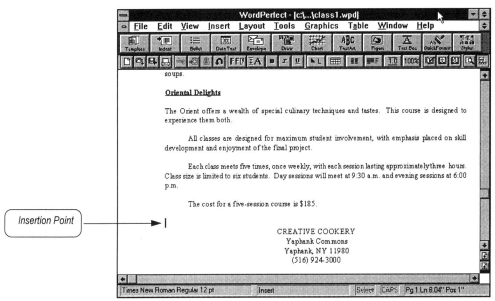

Figure 3 - 17

    You will underline the text you are about to type, and you will use the keyboard alternative to issue the underline command.

20. Press **CTRL+U** to start the underlining.

21. Type the following text: **Contact us at the following for further information or to enroll in a class:**

22. Press **CTRL + U** to end the underlining.

23. Press the **ENTER** key.

24. Choose **VIEW/Reveal Codes**.

    Figure 3 - 18 shows the line underlined in your document and the underline codes before and after it.

25. Recombine the screen.

    It is a good idea to stop at this point and save your document, so that you will not risk losing any of your work. You will give your document a different name, so that the original remains unchanged on your disk.

26. Choose **FILE/Save As**.

27. Save the file as **class2.wpd**

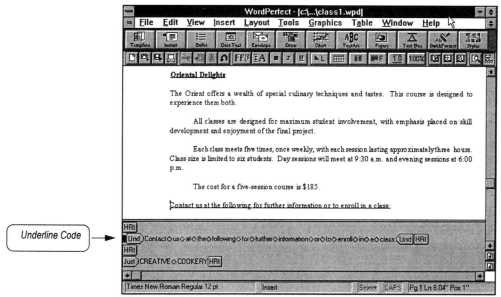

Figure 3 - 18

You will now use a different method to change the appearance of your text.

WORKING WITH FONTS

A font is a group of characters that have a common typeface or design. Fonts are organized in families by name. Each font family has its own special appearance or character. Font size is measured in points, with 72 points per inch. Font size can be changed by selecting a point size up to 100 points. The larger the point size you select, the larger your text will be.

You can change the typeface, size, and Appearance of your text by clicking on the **Font Face**, **Font Size**, and appearance buttons on the Power Bar. You can also use the **Font** dialog box to select a font name, select a point size, and select from a list of appearance options all at one time. The **Font** dialog box has more appearance options than the Power Bar. The **Font** dialog box also allows you to see a sample of the different fonts before you make your final choice. See Figure 3 - 19 for examples of different fonts.

This is an example of Times New Roman 12 pt.

This is an example of Times New Roman 16 pt.

This is an example of Times New Roman 16 pt Bold Italic

This is an example of Arial 14 pt

This is an example of Brush Script MT 18 pt

Figure 3 - 19

To use the Font dialog box to change fonts:

- Place the insertion point where you want the font change to begin.
- To change the font for a section of text, select the text you want to change.
- To change the font from that point forward, do not select any text.
- Click on **LAYOUT** in the Menu Bar to display the Layout Menu.
- Click on **FONT** to display the **Font** dialog box.
- Scroll through the fonts in the **Font Face** box and click on a font name.
- Click on a point size in the **Font Size** box.
- Click on any boxes in front of the **Appearance** options you want to change.
- Click on **OK** to close the **Font** dialog box.

To use the Power Bar to change fonts:

- Place the insertion point where you want the font change to begin.
- To change the font for a section of text, select the text you want to change.
- To change the font from that point forward, do not select any text.
- Click on the **Font Face** button on the Power Bar to change the font face.
- Scroll through the fonts and click on a font name.
- Click on the **Font Size** button on the Power Bar to change the font size.
- Click on a point size.

Activity 3.3: Using Fonts

In this part of the activity, you will use the Font dialog box to change sections of your text.

1. Place the Insertion point in front of the title line, **CREATIVE COOKERY**.

2. Select the line. See Figure 3 - 20.

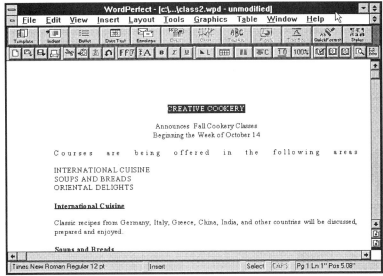

Figure 3 - 20

3. Choose **LAYOUT/Font.**

    *The **Font** dialog box shown in Figure 3 - 21 appears. The current font selection is highlighted in the **Font Face** box. Your list may be different from that shown in Figure 3 - 21, depending on your printer and the fonts installed on your computer. Windows provides fonts that can be used in WordPerfect for Windows. These are called True Type fonts and have TT in front of the font face name. If you do not see these True Type fonts or the fonts that you will need for the next part of the activity, see your laboratory instructor.*

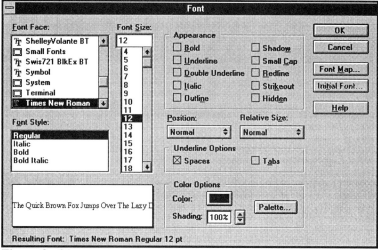

Figure 3 - 21

4. Use the scroll bar in the **Font Face** box to locate the **Arial** font and click to choose it.

5. Scroll until you locate 24 in the **Font Size** box and click to choose 24 points.

6. Click on **Bold** in the **Appearance** box.

7. Click on **Italic** in the **Appearance** box.

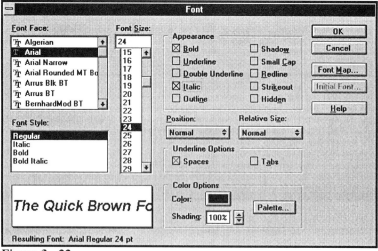

Figure 3 - 22

*An **x** appears in the box in front of an option to indicate that the option has been selected. The sample box at the bottom left of the dialog box shows you how your text will appear. See Figure 3 - 22.*

8. Click on some other options in the **Appearance** box and check the sample box to see the changes.

9. Click on the selected options to turn them off. Only **Bold** and **Italic** should remain selected.

   The hidden text option hides text and prevents it from being printed.

10. Click on **OK** to return to the document.

11. Figure 3 - 23 shows the font changes. The title line text is larger, bold, and in italics.

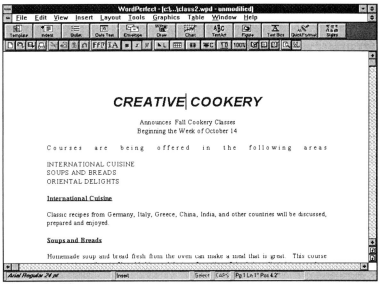

Figure 3 - 23

12. Place the insertion point anywhere in the title line.

    Notice the Font indicator on the status line at the bottom left of the screen. It should read Arial 24 pt. As you move through the document, the font indicator displays the fonts used to format your text.

13. Select the two title lines beginning, **Announces Fall Cookery Classes.** See Figure 3 - 24.

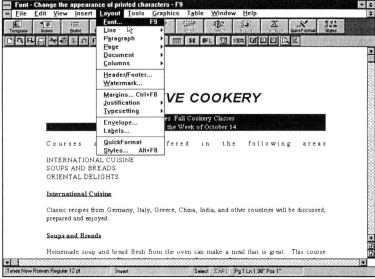

Figure 3 - 24

14. Choose **LAYOUT/Font**

15. Choose the Arial 18 point font.

16. Choose **Bold**.

17. Click on **OK** to return to the document.

18. Remove the highlighting

19. Select the line, **Courses are being offered in the following areas**.

20. Use the **Font** dialog box to change the text to Arial 14 point, **Bold**, and **Underline**.

    *Figure 3 - 25 shows the font changes. Another way to change only the font face and size is to use the Power Bar **Font** buttons.*

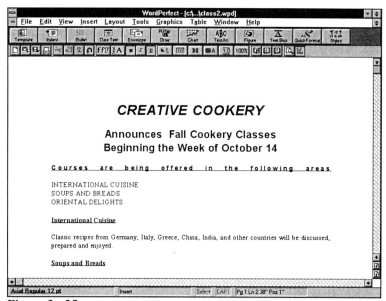

Figure 3 - 25

21. Place the insertion point in front of the first line in the name and address located under the announcement.

22. Select the four lines of the name and address. See Figure 3 - 26.

 23. Click on the **Font Face** button on the Power Bar.

24. Choose the Arial font.

 25. Click on the **Font Size** button on the Power Bar.

26. Choose 10 point.

27. Remove the highlighting.

    As with other text format changes, every time you make a font change you embed a hidden font code in your document. One way to remove the font changes from your text is to delete these font codes. You can also reselect the text and make another font change.

28. Select the name and address lines again.

29. Click on the **Font Size** button on the Power Bar.

30. Choose 14 point.

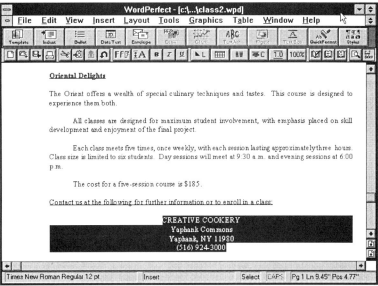

Figure 3 - 26

31. Remove the highlighting.

The Font for the text in the address lines has been changed to 14-point Arial. Place the insertion point in the address lines and check the Status Bar.

You will now use yet another method to emphasize your text.

CREATING A BULLET LIST

Bullets or numbers can be used to enumerate a list of items and to add emphasis to your text. You can add bullets or numbers to a list of items simply by selecting the items and clicking on the **Bullet** button on the Button Bar or by using the **Insert** menu. *WordPerfect* lets you select from a variety of bullet or numbering styles. Figure 3 - 27 shows some different bullet and number styles.

```
┌──────────────────────────────────┐
│  Bullet and Number Styles        │
│                                  │
│   •    Small Circle              │
│   ●    Large Circle              │
│   ►    Triangle                  │
│   ■    Square                    │
│   0.   Number                    │
│                                  │
└──────────────────────────────────┘
```

Figure 3 - 27

To create a bullet or number list:

•   Select the items.

•   Click on the **Bullet** button on the Button Bar.

•   Choose a bullet or number style by clicking on it.

•   Click on **OK** to return to the document.

Activity 3.4: Creating a Bullet List

In this activity, you will add bullets to the list of cooking classes at the top of the class announcement.

1. Place the insertion point in front of the first item in the list of cooking classes, **INTERNATIONAL CUISINE.**

2. Select the three items. See Figure 3 - 28.

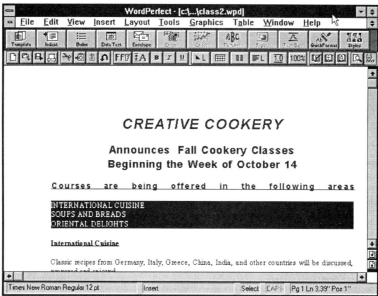

Figure 3 - 28

3. Click on the **Bullet** button on the Button Bar to display the **Bullets & Numbers** dialog box. See Figure 3 - 29.

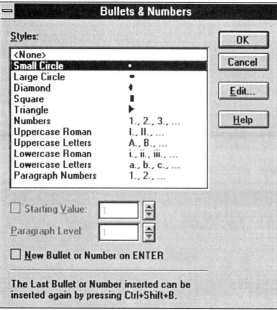

Figure 3 - 29

4. Choose the **Triangle bullet** by clicking on it.

5. Click on **OK** to return to the document.

6. Remove the highlighting.

   Figure 3 - 30 shows all three items with a triangle bullet in front of each.

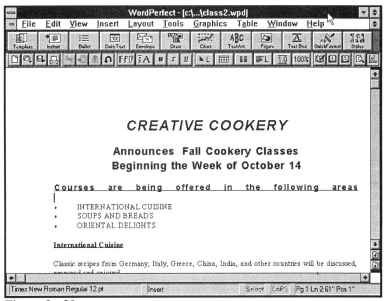

Figure 3 - 30

7. It is a good idea to stop at this point and save your document as **class2.wpd** again.

Other kinds of characters can also be inserted in your document for emphasis. In the next section of this project, you will learn how to insert these characters.

INSERTING SPECIAL CHARACTERS

Special characters are characters or symbols that are not available on the keyboard. *WordPerfect* provides almost 1,500 special characters arranged in character sets, including typographic, iconic, mathematical, scientific, and foreign-language characters. Not all special characters are available in all fonts, and not all printers can print all special characters.
Figure 3 - 31 shows some ways to use special characters.

☺ Yes, I would like to enroll in a cooking class!

☹ No, I am not interested in classes at this time.

© K. Daniels, 1994

Figure 3 - 31

To insert special characters:

- Place the insertion point where the special character is to appear.
- Click on **INSERT** in the Menu Bar to display the Insert Menu.
- Click on **Character** to display the *WordPerfect* **Characters** dialog box.
- Click on the **Character Set** down arrow.
- Choose a character set from the list.
- Click on a special character.
- Click on **Insert** or **Insert and Close**.

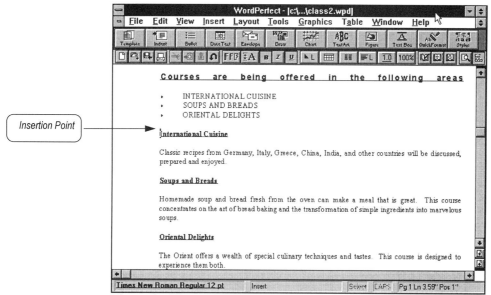

Figure 3 - 32

Activity 3.5: Inserting Special Characters

In this activity, you will place check marks in front of the three paragraph heading lines.

1. Place the insertion point in front of the first cooking class heading line, **International Cuisine**. See Figure 3 - 32.

2. Choose **INSERT/Character**.

3. The *WordPerfect* **Characters** dialog box shown in Figure 3 - 33 appears.

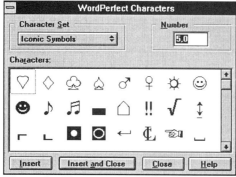

Figure 3 - 33

4. Click on the arrow on the **Character Set** button to display a list of available character sets.

5. Drag up or down to select the Iconic character set.

    A box with the special characters included in this character set will be displayed.

6. Scroll through the characters until you locate the check marks.

7. Click on the Check Mark, ✓ , to select it.

    A box will appear around the character.

8. Click on **Insert** to insert the check mark in your document.

    A check mark has been inserted in front of the cooking class name and the WordPerfect Characters dialog box remains open. You will add check marks to the other cooking class names before closing the dialog box. If the dialog box covers the text, you can move it by clicking on the Title Bar of the dialog box and dragging it to another section of the screen.

9. Place the insertion point in front of the second cooking class heading line, **Soups and Breads**.

10. The Check Mark should still be selected. If not, click on it.

11. Click on **Insert**.

12. Place the insertion point in front of the third cooking class heading line, **Oriental Delights.**

13. The Check Mark should still be selected.

14. Click on **Insert and Close**.

15. Figure 3 - 34 shows check marks in front of the three heading lines.

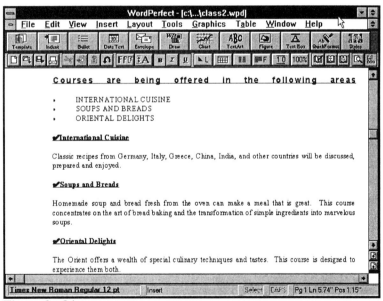

Figure 3 - 34

Activity 3.6: Saving and Printing the Document

1. **Save** the document as **class2.wpd** again.

2. Click on the **Print** button in the Power Bar.

3. Click on **Print** to print a copy of the document.

4. **Close** the document.

This completes the enhancement project.

KEY TERMS

Appearance	Italics
Bold	Justification
Bullet Button	Point Size
Character Set	Reveal Codes
Font Face	Special Characters
Font Size	Underline

INDEPENDENT PROJECTS

Independent Project 3.1: Enhancing Text

In this project you will add text enhancements to an announcement for winter cooking classes so that it looks like the one in Figure 3 - 35.

> **CREATIVE COOKERY**
>
> **Announces Winter Cookery Classes**
> **Beginning the Week of January 14**
>
> The following courses will be offered:
>
> ■ Introductory Baking Techniques
> ■ Advanced Baking Techniques
> ■ Cake Decorating
>
> All classes are designed to provide the student with techniques used in bread, pastry, and cake baking. The cake decorating class will concentrate on designing specialty cakes for birthdays, anniversaries, weddings, or other special occasions.
>
> Classes are designed for maximum student involvement, with emphasis placed on skill development and enjoyment of the final product.
>
> Each class meets three times, once weekly, with each session lasting approximately three hours. Class size is limited to 10 students. Classes meet on Wednesday evenings at 6:00 p.m. or Saturday at 9:30 a.m. The cost of a three-session course is $150.
>
> Mail in the following form to register for classes:
>
> --
>
> CREATIVE COOKERY
> Yaphank Commons
> Yaphank, NY 11980
>
> Name: _____   _____
>
> Address: _____   _____
>
> Check off the class for which you wish to register:
>
> ❑ Introductory Baking Techniques
>
> ❑ Advanced Baking Techniques
>
> ❑ Cake Decorating

Figure 3 - 35

1. Open the **WINTER** document.

2. Center the three title lines at the top of the document.

3. Change the font for the three title lines to Arial 18 pt. bold and italics.

4. Add square bullets to the list of cooking classes at the top of the document.

5. Center the three address lines in the registration form at the bottom of the document.

6. Use special characters (Iconic character set) to insert check-off boxes in front of the cooking classes in the registration form at the bottom of the announcement.

7. **Save** the document as **WINTER2** and **print** a copy.

8. **Close** the document.

Independent Project 3.2: Enhancing Text

In this project you will add text enhancements to an announcement for summer cooking classes so that it looks like the one in Figure 3 - 36.

CREATIVE COOKERY

Announces Summer Cookery Classes
Beginning the Week of June 4

The following courses will be offered:

- Succulent Seafood
- Sophisticated Tex Mex
- Picnic Fare

All classes are designed to provide the student with techniques used to prepare light, summer dishes and unusual picnic fare. The focus will be on providing creative warm-weather foods, many of which are portable. Safe warm-weather storage methods will also be covered.

Classes are designed for maximum student involvement, with emphasis placed on skill development and enjoyment of the final product.

Each class meets four times, once weekly, with each session lasting approximately three hours. Class size is limited to 12 students. Classes meet on Monday and Wednesday evenings at 6:00 p.m. or Saturday at 9:30 a.m.   The cost of a four-session course is $175.

For additional information or to register for classes, contact us at the following:

CREATIVE COOKERY
Yaphank Commons
Yaphank, NY 11980
(516) 924-3000

Figure 3 - 36

1. Open the **summer.wpd** document.

2. Center the three title lines at the top of the document.

3. Change the font for the first title line, **CREATIVE COOKERY**, to Arial 24 pt. bold.

4. Change the two title lines beginning, **Announces Summer...** to Arial 18 pt. bold.

5. Add diamond bullets to the list of cooking classes at the top of the document.

6. Change the text alignment for the paragraphs starting, **All classes are designed...** to full justified.

7. Center the four address lines at the bottom of the document.

8. **Save** the document as **summer2** and **print** a copy.

9. **Close** the document.

Independent Project 3.3: Enhancing Text

In this project you will use text enhancements to create on your own an attractive announcement for children's cooking classes. Use a variety of text alignments, fonts, and special characters. Include a bullet or number list.

- **Save** the document as **children** and **print** a copy.

- **Close** the document.

Independent Project 3.4: Enhancing Text

In this project you will add text enhancements to a memorandum, so that it looks like the one in Figure 3 - 37.

1. Open the **memspr.wpd** document.

2. Center the word **MEMORANDUM** and add bold and italics.

3. Add bold to the heading items: **TO: FROM: DATE:** and **SUBJECT**.

4. Add small circle bullets to the list of cooking classes at the bottom of the memorandum.

5. **Save** the document as **memspr2** and **print** a copy.

Independent Project 3.5: Enhancing Text

In this project you will use various text enhancements to create a letter to be sent out to prospective students, informing them of the upcoming winter cooking classes. Use the information in the **winter** document you printed in Independent Project 3.1 (Figure 3 - 35).

1. Use a variety of text enhancements.

2. **Save** the document as **letrwin** and **print** a copy.

MEMORANDUM

TO: All Staff

FROM: Deborah Kahlstrom
                  Scheduling Manager

DATE: January 22, 1995

SUBJECT: Spring Class Schedule

Now that the holiday class and catering schedule is behind us and the winter classes are underway, it is time to start thinking about the spring class and catering schedule. I would like to hold a meeting to discuss class and teaching schedules on February 3 at 10:00 a.m. in Room 203. Below is a tentative list of classes. Please bring your suggestions to the meeting.

- The Spring Buffet
- Indian Curries
- Cooking on the Barbeque

Figure 3 - 37

Lesson 4 Formatting Documents

Objectives:

In this lesson you will learn how to:

- Change document margins
- Change line spacing
- Set tab stops
- Use paragraph indents

- Use the Ruler Bar
- Insert a page break
- Combine documents

PROJECT: A NEWSLETTER ARTICLE

Creative Cookery produces a quarterly newsletter with food-related articles, recipes, restaurant reviews, and cooking tips. The current issue is devoted to cooking with herbs and spices and begins with an article discussing the differences between an herb and a spice. Your job today is to open this article and use *WordPerfect's* formatting features to improve its appearance. *WordPerfect* comes with certain preset document formats. In this project you will learn how to change these formats. Figure 4 - 1 shows the finished article.

CHANGING MARGINS WITH THE MARGINS DIALOG BOX

Page margins are the white space at the top, bottom, left, and right of the text on a page. The default margins are 1 inch all around and are set for a standard sheet of paper, which is 8.5 inches wide and 11 inches long. You can change all the margins with the **Margins** dialog box. You can also change just the left and right margins with the Ruler Bar.

To change page margins with the Margins dialog box:

- Place the insertion point where the margin change is to be made.
- Click on **LAYOUT** in the Menu Bar to display the **Layout** menu.
- Click on **MARGINS** to display the **Margins** dialog box.
- Type the new margin settings.
- Click on **OK** to return to the document.

HERB OR SPICE

What is the difference between an herb and a spice? Herbs are the leaves of certain

plants such as parsley, tarragon, rosemary, or thyme and are very aromatic. Spices are the seeds

such as pepper, mustard, or fennel; nuts such as nutmeg or allspice; or bark such as cinnamon.

Both herbs and spices are used to enhance the flavor of meats, fish and poultry.

The following recipe is loaded with herbs and spices. Served with a fresh loaf of
bread and crisp white wine, it makes a perfect lunch or light dinner. Try it, I
think you'll like it!

SAVORY FISH STEW

3 strips of bacon, 2 cloves of garlic, minced
1 cup each onion, green pepper, carrot, celery, coarsely chopped
1 tsp. each fresh basil, thyme, rosemary, parsley (1/2 tsp. dried), 1 bay leaf
1 tsp. worcestershire sauce, 1/2 cup white wine, 3 cups chicken stock, 1 1/2 lbs. fresh cod

Instructions:

In a large pot, saute the bacon until it starts to crisp. Add the vegetables and the herbs and stir.
    Turn the heat to high and add the worcestershire sauce.

Add the wine and stir to deglaze the pot. Add the stock and the tomatoes. Simmer until the
    carrots are tender. Cut the fish into chunks and add. Cook 5 minutes.

Also in this issue:

Figure 4 - 1

Activity 4.1 - Changing Margins with the Margins Dialog Box

In this activity, you will change the top and left margins of the article document.

1. Open the **spice.wpd** document.

2. Place the insertion point at the beginning of the document.

3. Choose **LAYOUT/Margins.**

*The **Margins** dialog box (Figure 4 - 2) appears. The current page margins are displayed and the left margin setting in the left margin text box is highlighted. You can type the new margin settings or click on the up or down arrow in the text box to increase or decrease the margin settings. The view panel at the right will display an example of the new margin settings.*

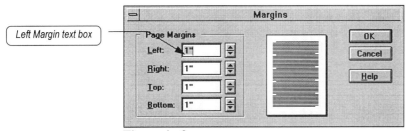

Figure 4 - 2

1. Type 1.5 in the **Left margin** text box.

2. Press the **TAB** key two times to highlight the top margin setting.

3. Type 1.5 in the **Top margin** text box.

4. Click on **OK** to return to the document.

   Look at the status bar at the bottom right of the screen. You should see the new line and character positions.

8. Reveal the codes.

   You should see the left and top margin codes shown in Figure 4 - 3. As with appearance changes, all formatting changes you make in your document are controlled by hidden codes. The formatting codes are usually placed where you make the format change; however, format codes that affect pages or paragraphs are automatically placed at the beginning of the page or paragraph with the Auto Code placement feature.

9. Recombine the screen.

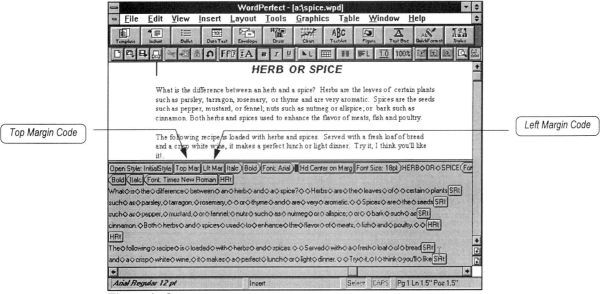

Figure 4 - 3

In the next section of this project, you will learn to use a different method to change just the left and right margins.

THE RULER BAR

The Ruler Bar can be displayed at the top of the screen. The Ruler Bar displays the left and right margin markers in the upper band. It also displays the tab stop positions as triangular marks that appear below the scale.

To display the Ruler Bar:

• Click on **VIEW** in the Menu Bar to display the **View** menu.

• Click on **Ruler Bar** to display the Ruler Bar at the top of the screen.

To use the Ruler Bar to change the left and right margins:

• Click on the margin marker on the upper band of the Ruler Bar.

• Drag the margin marker to the new margin position.

Activity 4.2 - Displaying and Using the Ruler Bar to Change Margins

1. Choose **VIEW/Ruler Bar**.

    You should see the Ruler Bar with the margin markers and tab markers shown in Figure 4 - 4.

Figure 4 - 4

2. Click on the left margin marker and drag it back to the 1-inch position on the scale.

    When you click on a margin marker, a vertical broken line appears. As you drag the margin marker, you will see the new margin position on the status bar at the bottom right of the screen.

3. Click on the right margin marker and drag it to the 7-inch position on the scale. Check the status bar as you drag the margin marker.

4. Drag the right margin marker back to the 7.5 inch position on the scale.

   Your left and right margins should be back at the default of 1 inch. The left margin marker should be at 1 inch on the scale and the right margin marker should be at 7.5 inches on the scale.

   In the next section of this project, you will make additional changes to the document's format.

CHANGING LINE SPACING

You can increase the amount of white space between the lines of text by increasing the line spacing--for example, one-and-a half or double spacing. The default line spacing is single spacing. Place the insertion point where you want the line spacing change to start. To change the line spacing of a section of your document, first select the text. The rest of the document will be unchanged. You can use the **Line Spacing** dialog box or the **Line Spacing** button on the Power Bar to change line spacing.

To change line spacing with the Line Spacing dialog box:

- Place the insertion point where the line spacing change is to be made or select the text.
- Click on **LAYOUT** in the menu bar to display the **Layout** menu.
- Click on **LINE** to display the Line format menu.
- Click on **SPACING** to display the **Line Spacing** dialog box.
- Type a number in the **Line Spacing** text box.
- Click on **OK** to return to the document screen.

To change line spacing with the Power Bar:

- Place the insertion point where the line spacing is to change or select the text.
- Click on the **Line Spacing** button on the Power Bar and drag to the desired spacing.

Activity 4.3 - Changing Line Spacing

In this activity, you will explore different ways to change the line spacing of your document. At the end of the activity, the line spacing for the first paragraph of the article will be double spaced and the remainder of the document will be single spaced. First, you will change the line spacing for the entire document to double spacing.

1. Place the insertion point at the beginning of the document.

2. Choose **LAYOUT/Line,Spacing**

   *The **Line Spacing** dialog box shown in Figure 4 - 5 appears. The current line spacing is displayed in the **Spacing** text box. You can change the line spacing by typing a number in the text box or clicking on the arrow to increase or decrease the spacing. The sample box to the right will display a sample of the line spacing.*

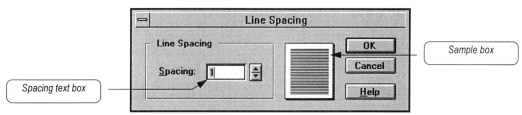

Figure 4 - 5

3. Type **2** in the **Spacing** text box.

4. Click on **OK** to return to the document.

5. Scroll through the document.

    Figure 4 - 6 shows the document with double spacing. A line spacing format code has been embedded at the beginning of your document and all text following this code until the end of the document is double spaced. In the next section of this activity, you will return the line spacing to single.

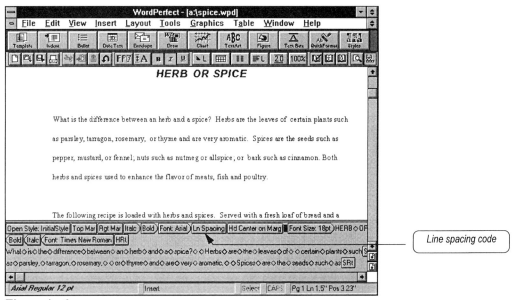

Figure 4 - 6

6. Place the insertion point at the beginning of the document and reveal the codes.

7. Locate the line spacing code and delete it.

8. Recombine the screen.

    *Your text should now be single spaced again. An alternate way to return to single spacing would be to place the insertion point at the beginning of the document and use the line spacing dialog box to set the line spacing to single. In the next part of this activity, you will change the spacing of only the first paragraph to double spacing and you will use the **Line Spacing** button on the Power Bar. Although the Power Bar is a more efficient way to change the line spacing, you have only single, one-and-a-half, and double spacing readily available. To get any other spacing, you still need to use the line spacing dialog box.*

9. Place the insertion point at the beginning of the first paragraph, **What is the difference**...

10. Select the first paragraph. See Figure 4 - 7.

Figure 4 - 7

11. Click on the **Line Spacing** button on the Power Bar and drag down to 2.0.

   The first paragraph is double spaced, while the remainder of the document remains unchanged. Figure 4 - 8 shows how your document should appear.

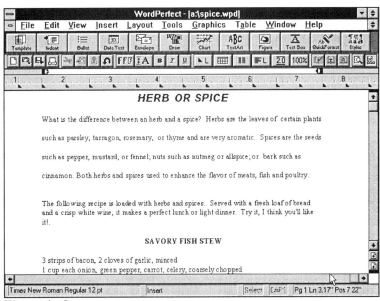

Figure 4 - 8

You will continue to change the document formats by changing the default tab stops. Before continuing, however, it is a good idea to save your work.

12. Use **Save As** to save the file as **spice2.wpd**

CHANGING TAB STOPS

Tab stops are used to move text over to a specific position on the line, to line up columns, and to indent paragraphs. Default tab stops are set every .5 inches. These default tab positions can be changed. Pressing the **TAB** key moves the insertion point to the right each time it is pressed. The Ruler Bar displays the tab stop positions as triangular marks that appear below the scale. The shape of the tab mark indicates the type of tab stop. *WordPerfect* provides eight different types of tab stops: Left, right, center, decimal, dot left, dot center, dot right, and dot decimal. The default tab stop is left. The dot tab stops automatically insert leader dots between columns. You can see the different types of tab stops in Figure 4 - 9

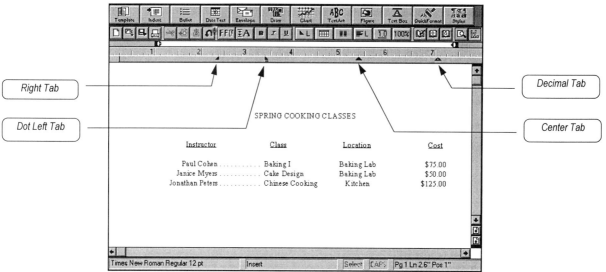

Figure 4 - 9

Tab stops can be set in a relative position or an absolute position. Relative tab stops are set a certain distance from the left margin. If you change the left margin, the relative tab stops will always remain the same distance from the left margin. Absolute tab stops are set a certain distance from the left edge of the page. They will not change position if you change the left margin. By default, tab stops are set in a relative position.

Tab stops can be set with the **Tab Set** dialog box and with the **Tab Set** button on the Power Bar and the Ruler Bar. A hidden tab set code is placed in your text and the tab stops are changed from that point forward. You can have multiple tab stop changes in a document.

To set tab stops with the Tab Set dialog box:

- Place the insertion point where the tab stop change is to be made.
- Click on **LAYOUT** to display the **Layout** menu.
- Click on **LINE** to display the **Line Format** menu.
- Click on **TAB SET** to display the **Tab Set** dialog box.
- Click on **Clear All** to remove existing tab stops.
- Select the type of tab using the **Type** selection box.
- Choose Relative (left margin) or Absolute (left edge) position.
- Type the location of the tab in the **Position** text box.

- Click on **Set**.
- Repeat to set the remaining tab stops.
- Click on **OK** to return to the document.

To set tab stops with the Ruler Bar:

- If the Ruler Bar is not displayed, click on the **Tab Set** button on the Power Bar and choose **Set Tabs**. If the Ruler Bar is displayed, go to the next step.
- Click on the **Tab Set** button on the Power Bar.
- Choose **Clear All Tabs**.
- Click on the **Tab Set** button on the Power Bar.
- Choose the type of tab stop you want to set. For example, Right.
- To set tab stops, click underneath the position on the scale line where the tab is to be set.
- To move a tab stop, click on the tab marker on the scale line and drag it horizontally to another location.
- To delete a tab stop, click on the tab marker and drag it off the scale line.

Activity 4.4 - Setting and Using Tab Stops

In the first section of this activity, you will use the **TAB** key to indent the first line of the first paragraph .5 inches. Since the default tab stops are set every .5 inches, you do not need to change the tab stop positions. Then you will change the default tab stops and add some tabular columns at the end of the document.

1. Display the Ruler Bar, if necessary, to display existing tab stops.

2. Place the insertion point at the beginning of the first paragraph beginning, **What is the difference**... and press the **TAB** key.

   The first line of the paragraph is now indented to the first tab stop location, 1.5 inches

3. Place the insertion point at the end of the document. See Figure 4 - 10.

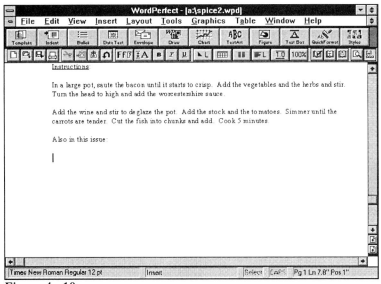

Figure 4 - 10

4. Choose **LAYOUT/Line,Tab Set.**

   *The **Tab Set** dialog box shown in Figure 4 - 11 appears.*

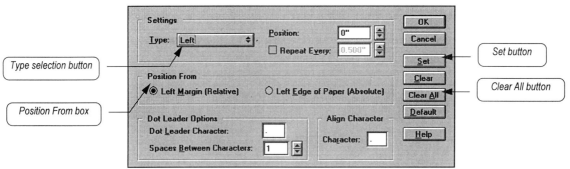

Figure 4 - 11

5. Click on **Clear All** to remove the existing tab stops.

   You will set a Right tab stop for the first column. Everything in this column will be aligned on the right side of the column.

6. Click on the arrow on the **Type** selection button and drag to select Right.

7. In the **Position From** box, click on Left Edge of Paper (Absolute)

8. Type **4** in the **Position** text box.

9. Click on **Set**.

   You have changed the default position from relative to the left margin, to absolute. The tab stop you just set is 4 inches from the left edge. A right tab marker appears at the 4-inch position on the scale. You will now set a center tab for the second column.

10. Click on the arrow in the **Type** selection box and drag to select Center.

11. Type **5** in the **Position** text box.

12. Click on **Set**.

   A Center tab marker appears at the 5-inch position on the scale. Everything in this column will be centered. You will now set a Left tab with leader dots for the third column. Leader dots are dots inserted between tab columns to help guide the reader's eye across the line.

13. Click on the arrow on the **Type** selection button and drag to select Dot Left.

14. Type **7** in the **Position** text box.

15. Click on **Set**.

   A Dot Left tab marker appears at the 7-inch position on the scale line. Leader dots will automatically be inserted between the second and third columns as you type.

16. Click on **OK** to return to the document.

   Your Ruler Bar should look like the one in Figure 4 - 12. If it does not, reveal the codes and locate the Tab Set code. You can delete the code by clicking on the code and dragging it out of the Reveal Codes window into the document window. Then repeat steps 4 - 16 in Activity 4.4 to reset your tab stops.

17. Type the text in Figure 4 - 13 at the bottom of your document. Remember to press the **TAB** key at the beginning of each column item and press the **ENTER** key at the end of each line.

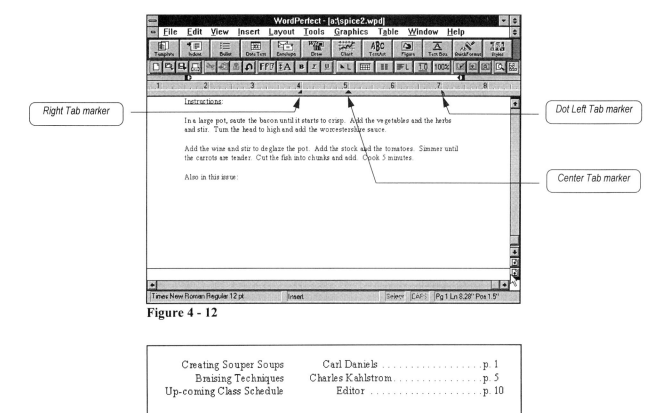

Figure 4 - 12

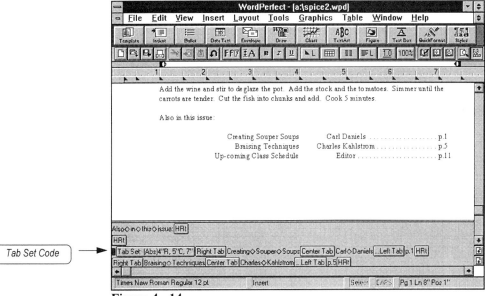

Figure 4 - 13

Notice that in the first column the text aligns at the right side of the column. The text in the second column is centered. The text in the third column is aligned at the left side and leader dots have been inserted between the second and third columns. A Tab Set code has been embedded above the text columns. See Figure 4 - 14.

Figure 4 - 14

In the next activity, you will learn how to modify your tab stops, using the Ruler Bar.

Activity 4.5 - Modifying Tab Stops with the Ruler Bar

When you wish to change current tab positions, reveal the codes and place the insertion point immediately after the tab set code. If the insertion point is not immediately after the tab set code, you will embed a new tab set code in the document rather than modifying the original code.

1. Display the Ruler Bar if necessary

2. Reveal the codes

3. Place the insertion point immediately after the Tab Set code. See Figure 4 - 15

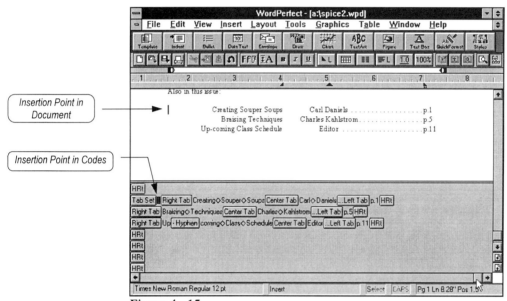

Figure 4 - 15

When you use the Ruler Bar to modify existing tabs, you will click on the tab stop marker you want to move. A broken line will appear. You will then drag the tab stop marker horizontally across the scale to reposition the tab stop.

4. Click on the Right tab marker at the 4-inch position on the scale and drag it to 3.5 inches.

    The text column will move as you drag the tab stop code. See Figure 4 - 16 for the new tab settings.

5. Recombine the screen.

    In the next section of this activity, you will use the Ruler Bar to add and remove tab stops.

6. Place the insertion point underneath the columns. See Figure 4 - 17.

7. Click on the right tab marker at the 3.5-inch position on the scale line and drag it down to the document area to remove it.

8. Click on the Center tab marker at the 5-inch position on the scale line and drag it down to the document area to remove it.

9. Remove the dot left tab marker at the 7-inch position.

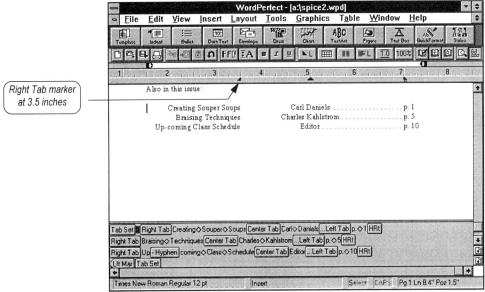

Figure 4 - 16

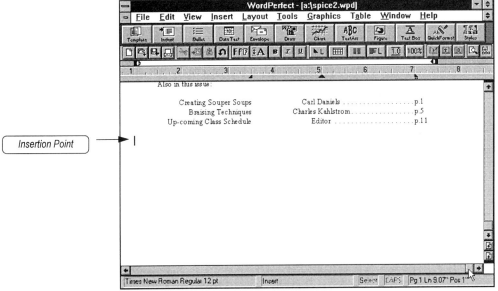

Figure 4 - 17

*The Ruler Bar has no tab markers. In the next part of this activity, you will set left tab stops at the 1.5-inch position and the 2-inch position with the **Tab Set** button on the Power Bar and the Ruler Bar. Before setting tab stops, confirm that the **Tab Set** button on the Power Bar shows the triangle and letter for the type of tab stop you are setting. The last type of tab stop set is the type displayed on the **Tab Set** button.*

 10. Click on the **Tab Set** button on the Power Bar and drag to select Left.

11. Point to the 1.5-inch position on the bottom bar of the Ruler Bar and click with the left mouse button.

A left tab marker should appear at 1.5 inches. If it does not, try again, keeping the pointer below the line underneath the scale numbers.

12. Point to the 2-inch position on the bottom bar of the Ruler Bar and click with the left mouse button.

13. A left tab marker should appear at 2 inches. Your Ruler Bar should look like the one in Figure 4 - 18.

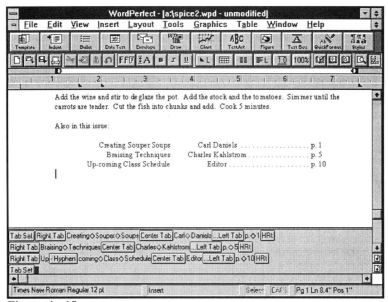

Figure 4 - 18

It is a good idea to stop at this point and save your document, so that you will not risk losing any of your work.

14. Save the document as **spice2.wpd** again.

In the next section of this project, you will learn how to change paragraph formats.

INDENTING PARAGRAPHS

You have used the **TAB** key to type text in columns. You have also used the **TAB** key to indent the first line of a paragraph. There are occasions, however, when you want to indent an entire paragraph. For example, it is common practice to indent long quotations five spaces in from the left and right margins. Indents can also be used to emphasize text or to type lists of items.

You can use the paragraph indent feature to indent an entire paragraph in three different ways: Left indent, double indent, and hanging indent. Left Indent indents the paragraph from the left margin. Double Indent indents the paragraph from both the left and right margins. Hanging Indent leaves the first line at the left margin and indents the remainder of the paragraph. Paragraphs are indented to the next tab stop. The easiest way to indent paragraphs from the left margin only is to use the **Indent** button on the Button Bar. You can also use the Layout and Paragraph menus to choose other indent styles.

*Figure 4 - 19 shows the three different kinds of indents that **WordPerfect** provides. These indents have many different uses, including quotations or land descriptions, enumerations, or for text emphasis.*

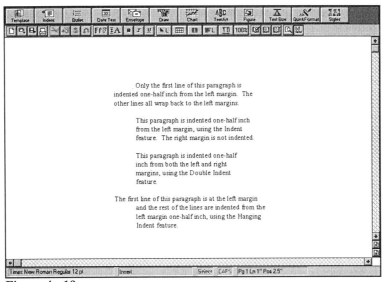

Figure 4 - 19

Indenting paragraphs:

- Place the insertion point at the beginning of the paragraph you want to indent.
- Choose **LAYOUT/Paragraph**.
- Click on **Indent**, **Hanging Indent**, or **Double Indent**

Activity 4.6 - Indenting Paragraphs

You will use the Double Indent feature to add emphasis to the second paragraph in the **spice2.wpd** document and the Hanging Indent for the two instructions in the recipe.

1. Place the insertion point at the beginning of the second paragraph beginning, **The following recipe is loaded**...See Figure 4 - 20.

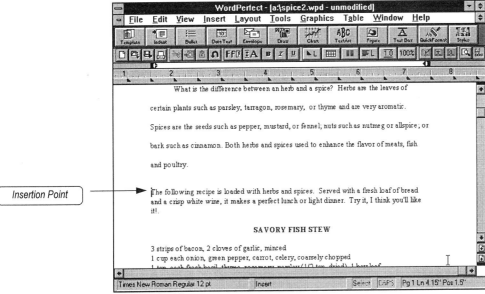

Figure 4 - 20

2. Choose **LAYOUT/Paragraph**.

   The Paragraph menu shown in Figure 4 - 21 appears.

Figure 4 - 21

3. Click on **Double Indent**.

   Figure 4 - 22 shows the second paragraph indented .5 inches from both the left and right margins.

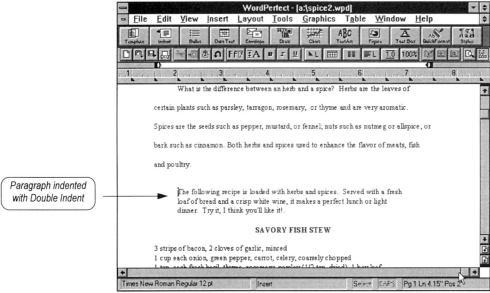

Figure 4 - 22

4. Place the insertion point at the beginning of the first recipe instruction beginning, **In a large pot...** See Figure 4 - 23.

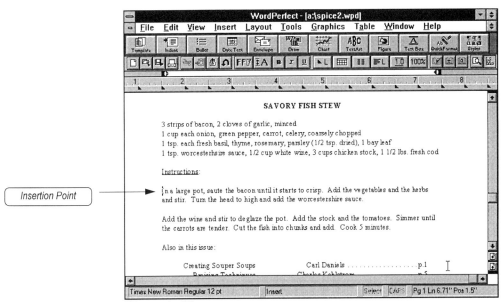

Figure 4 - 23

5. Choose **LAYOUT/Paragraph,Hanging Indent**.

   Figure 4 - 24 shows the first instruction line with the first line at the left margin and the next line indented.

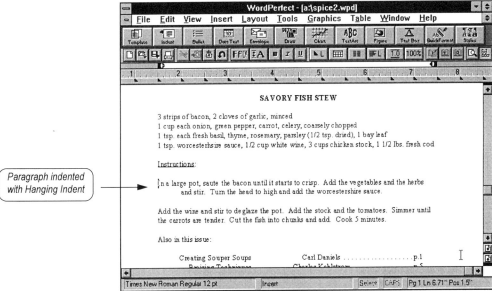

Figure 4 - 24

6. Use the Hanging Indent feature to indent the second instruction line beginning, **Add the wine and stir**...

   *Indent formatting codes have been placed at the beginning of each of the paragraphs that you indented. A **[Hd LeftRight Ind]** code should appear at the beginning of the third paragraph and **[Hd Left Ind]** and **[Hd Back Tab]** codes at the beginning of each of the instruction paragraphs. If you wanted to remove the indents, you would delete these codes from your document.*

7. **Save** the document on your disk as **spice2.wpd** again.

8. **Print** a copy of the article and compare it with Figure 4 - 1.

In the next section of this activity, you will insert a page break and combine another article with the spice article.

PAGE BREAKS

WordPerfect provides two types of page breaks: Soft page break and hard page break. When the text you are typing fills a page, *WordPerfect* automatically inserts a Soft Page Break code. If you want to open a new page before a page is filled, you can insert a Hard Page Break code.

To Insert a Page Break:

*   Place the insertion point where you want to open the new page.

*   Choose **INSERT/Page Break** or press the **CTRL+ENTER** keys.

Activity 4.7: Inserting a Page Break

1. Place the insertion point at the end of the document. See Figure 4 - 25.

    The page break will be made at the insertion point

2. Choose **INSERT/Page Break**

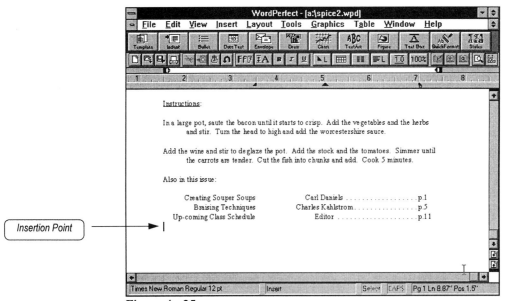

Figure 4 - 25

A horizontal line appears on the screen. When your insertion point is below this line, the status bar at the bottom right of the screen will indicate that you are on page 2. When your insertion point is above this line, the status bar will indicate that you are on page 1.
Figure 4 - 26 shows the Hard Page Break code that has been embedded in your document. If you want to remove a page break, reveal the codes and delete the Hard Page Break code.
Soft Page Break codes cannot be removed.

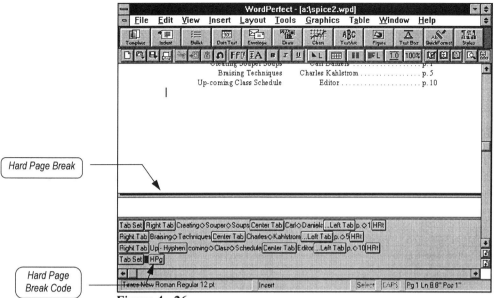

Figure 4 - 26

COMBINING DOCUMENTS

You can combine documents easily with *WordPerfect*. *WordPerfect* allows you to combine the current document with another *WordPerfect* document or a document created with another program. In this part of the project, you will combine another article created with *WordPerfect* with the **spice2.wpd** article.

To Combine Documents:

- Position the insertion point where the document is to be placed.

- Choose **INSERT/File** to display the **Insert File** dialog box.

- Select the file from the file list.

- Click on **Insert**.

- Click on **Yes** to return to the document.

Activity 4.8: Combining Documents

1. Position the insertion point on page 2.

2. Choose **INSERT/File**.

   *The **Insert File** dialog box showing the current directory and list of files similar to that shown in* Figure 4 - 27 *appears*

3. Select the **herb.wpd** document from the file list.

4. Click on **Insert**.

5. Click on **Yes**.

   *The **herb** article is now placed on page 2.*

6. Use **Save As** to save the document as **spice3.wpd**.

7. **Print** a copy.

8. **Close** the File.

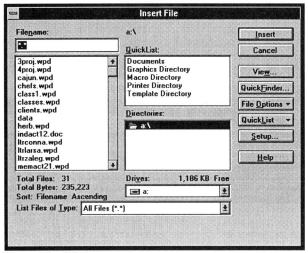

Figure 4 - 27

This completes the formatting project.

KEY TERMS

Combining Documents	Line Format
Double Indent	Line Format Menu
Hanging Indent	Line Spacing
Indent	Page Break
Layout	Ruler Bar
Leader Dots	Save As

INDEPENDENT PROJECTS

Independent Project 4.1: Formatting a Document

In this project you will open and format a newsletter article so that it looks like the one in Figure 4 - 28.

1. Open the **herb.wpd** document.

2. Change the top margin to 1.5 inches.

3. Change the line spacing for the paragraph beginning, **Herbs can be a wonderful...** to single spacing and use the Double Indent feature to indent the paragraph.

4. Change the line spacing for the recipe and instructions to single spacing.

5. Use the Hanging Indent feature to indent the two instruction lines of the recipe.

HERBS

Herbs have been used to flavor foods for thousands of years. Herbs have also been valued for their medicinal properties and have even been used as charms.

The ancient Greeks used parsley to cure stomach aches. Rosemary was used in the Middle Ages as a tranquilizer. Mustard seeds have also been very popular throughout history. Shakespeare even included references to mustard in his plays!

Today, we still value herbs for their ability to enhance the flavor of our foods, as well as for their medicinal properties. Many "natural food" stores sell herbal preparations.

Herbs can be a wonderful way to add variety to otherwise monotonous recipes. Here is a recipe for an unusual way to prepare potatoes:

HERBED POTATOES

1 lb. red or white boiling potatoes
1/4 cup olive oil, 1 tsp. salt
2 tsp. fresh chopped herbs (can include rosemary, parsley, thyme or any combination you prefer)

Slice the potatoes in half and boil them for approximately 10 minutes, or until they are about half cooked. While the potatoes are boiling, mix the olive oil, salt and herbs in a bowl. Drain the potatoes well and place in the bowl with the oil mixture. Marinate the potatoes for at least 1 hr.

Thread the potatoes on skewers and grill them on a hot grill until golden brown on the outside and soft on the inside.

ONE-DAY COOKING CLASS SCHEDULE

Pasta Making . . . . January 14
Chinese Cooking I . . . . January 21
Chinese Cooking II . . . . February 11
Advanced Baking Techniques . . . . March 5

Figure 4 - 28

6. Change the font for the article title, **HERBS**, to Arial 14 pt. bold.

7. Add bold to the recipe title, **HERBED POTATOES**.

8. Place the insertion point at the end of the document.

9. Clear the existing tab stops.

10. Set the following tab stops in the Left edge of paper (absolute) position: Right tab stop at 4 inches; dot left tab stop at 5 inches.

11. Type the tabular columns shown in Fig. 4-29 at the bottom of the document.

12. **Save** the document as **herb2.wpd** and **print** a copy.

```
ONE-DAY COOKING CLASS SCHEDULE

Pasta Making . . . . . . . . . . .January 14
Chinese Cooking I . . . . . . . . . .January 21
Chinese Cooking II . . . . . . . . . .February 11
Advanced Baking Techniques . . . . . . . . . . .March 5
```

Figure 4 - 29

Independent Project 4.2: Combining Documents

In this project, you will open a new page in a document and insert a file.

1. Open the **herb2.wpd** document.

2. Place the insertion point at the end of the document and open a new page.

3. Insert the **winter.wpd** document on page two.

4. **Save** the document as **herbwint.wpd** and **print** a copy.

5. **Close** the document.

Independent Project 4.3: Formatting and Combining Documents

In this project you will type a letter of response to a request for information about the fall cooking classes and combine it with an announcement document. You will start by typing the letterhead information at the top and then you will type the letter in block format.

1. Change the top, left, and right margins to 1.5 inches.

2. Type the letter shown in Figure 4 - 30. Use the Arial 18 pt. and 14 pt. fonts and bold for the return address. Use the Times New Roman 12 pt. font for the letter. Center the return address.

3. **Open** a new page.

4. Insert the **announce.wpd** document on page two.

5. **Save** the letter as **letrgpt.wpd** and **print** a copy.

6. **Close** the document.

CREATIVE COOKERY
Yaphank Commons
Yaphank, NY 11980

Mr. Robert Brown
23 Raimond Street
Yaphank, NY 11980

Dear Mr. Brown:

Thank you for your inquiry about our fall cooking classes. The enclosed announcement describes the classes offered this fall. As you can see, we are offering an exciting series, covering international and down-home favorites.

These classes are filling rapidly. Please call us at (516)555-1234 as soon as possible to register for one or more classes. If you have an questions, as for Greg.

Sincerely,

Gregory A. Zaleta
Vice President

GZ

Enclosure

Figure 4 - 30

Independent Project 4.4: Formatting and Combining Documents

In this project you will create a letter of response to a request for information about the summer cooking classes and combine it with an announcement. Use the information in the **summer.wpd** document shown in Figure 4 - 31

CREATIVE COOKERY

**Announces Summer Cookery Classes
Beginning the Week of June 4**

<u>**The following courses will be offered:**</u>

- Succulent Seafood
- Sophisticated Tex Mex
- Picnic Fare

All classes are designed to provide the student with techniques used to prepare light, summer dishes and unusual picnic fare. The focus will be on providing creative warm-weather foods, many of which are portable. Safe warm-weather storage methods will also be covered.

Classes are designed for maximum student involvement, with emphasis placed on skill development and enjoyment of the final product.

Each class meets four times, once weekly, with each session lasting approximately three hours. Class size is limited to 12 students. Classes meet on Monday and Wednesday evenings at 6:00 p.m. or Saturday at 9:30 a.m. The cost of a four-session course is $175.

For additional information or to register for classes, contact us at the following:

**CREATIVE COOKERY
Yaphank Commons
Yaphank, NY 11980
(516) 924-3000**

Figure 4 - 31

1. Start by typing a letterhead at the top and then type the letter in block format. Use various formats and text enhancements. Use today's date and your name as the author in the letter closing.

2. **Open** a new page in the document.

3. Insert the **summer.wpd** document on page two.

4. **Save** the document with an appropriate name and **print** a copy.

Independent Project 4.5: Formatting an Article

In this project you will research one of the following topics: Computer use in the food industry; electronic recipe programs; word processors, graphics, and menu preparation; or a topic approved by your instructor.

1. Prepare a brief newsletter article, using various formats and text enhancements.

2. Save the document with an appropriate name and print a copy.

Lesson 5 # Working with Multiple Page Documents and Graphics

Objectives:

In this lesson you will learn how to:

- Create a research report following the MLA style guidelines.

- Type a header containing a page number into text.

- Insert a file into an existing document.

- Create a footnote and a citation.

- Place a graphic within the document.

PROJECT: CREATING A RESEARCH REPORT WITH GRAPHICS

WordPerfect for Windows is a full-feature word processor that allows you to integrate text and graphics. You no longer need to leave your word processing software to create professional looking newsletters and business and research reports. Desktop publishing features such as graphics, charts, and page layout are available in *WordPerfect* and allow you to enhance the appearance of your documents.

In this project, you will learn how to use the power of *WordPerfect* to create a research report that follows the MLA (Modern Language Association of America) style guidelines. You are a client of Creative Cookery and you are taking a course entitled Restaurant Management that is being taught this semester by Brian Dorrian. Your instructor asks you to prepare a research report on a restaurant named Carl Victor's. You will create this report using the MLA style guidelines. By following these guidelines, the reports of all of the students in the class will have the same format and appearance. Your final report will look like the report in Figure 5 - 1.

STYLES OF RESEARCH REPORTS

There are many types of research and business report style guidelines. *The Chicago Manual of Style*, the *MLA Handbook for Writers of Research Papers*, and the *Publication Manual of the American Psychological Association* are the three most popular research report style guidelines. When you prepare a research report, it is important to understand the report style that your instructor expects you to follow and apply its guidelines consistently as you create your report.

Each style uses slightly different guidelines for creating footnotes, end notes, figures, and page formatting. The MLA style is followed by most organizations for research reports. Many of the format requirements set by MLA are default format settings within *WordPerfect*. However, there are several format settings that are unique and require a modification to *WordPerfect*'s default settings.

Works Cited

United States, Bureau of Census, Current Population Reports, E

P50-174 and P20--485.

Author's Name 1

Your Full Name

Professor Brian Dorrian

Introduction to Restaurant Management 101

Today's Date

Carl Victor's is a a 60-seat, competitively-priced family restaurant which serves a *Businessperson's Lunch*[1] and dinner. The main menu has 10 to 15 staple items of American novelle and Continental dishes. This menu is augmented by an extensive specialty board, reflecting the more fanciful whims of the owner. The restaurant and lounge is located in the Stony Brook area of New York. This area of Suffolk County on the north shore of Long Island has doubled in population in the past ten years, with 67 percent of that increase in families with annual gross incomes of $60,000 or over (US Bureau of Census 1990, 320).

This increase is accounted for by the enormous amount of corporate expansion taking place all over central Long Island. Giant office centers are rising out of the sand like chrome and

...ully leased before the construction crews arrive on the scene.

...s sites in this target area is very good. Prospective sites are

...n walking distance of, these huge office complexes that rival

...space. The network of modern roadways being built with the

...tor's quite convenient and very accessible to the half dozen or

...nd villages.

...apture mood of the area. It has an easy to read sign that has

...a quick lunch that is specially priced to attract a particular

Your Name 3

This frees the chef, most cooks, and other help from lunch-related duties so that they may prepare for the more exacting dinner. The typical lunch includes a fresh spinach salad with house dressing, a large bowl of Savory Fish Stew served with crusty rye bread and a glass of house wine. This is a fast, easy and profitable lunch menu.

The fixed menu consists of two sizes of prime steak, custom-made burgers served on hard rolls, and a large appetizer selection.

The dinner menu consists of ten to 15 American and Continental dishes. The catagories of meat, fish, poultry and vegetarian are included but reflect the special preparation that only Carl Victor's can present.

It is important that the resturant have a visual recognition with its customers as well as name recognition. For this reason, a company logo has been carfully selected. The company logo is a bird in flight. It depicts the casual, lighthearted mood of the resturant. It

Figure 1 Company Logo

also promise to connect the customers with the elegant appearance of a bird in motion.

Family Style Service

The serving bowls and platters have an asthetic appeal to the customer. This method of services also reduces wast and makes portioning and plating easier and more efficient for the kitchen. The idea of have a home-cooked family style dinner, with all the elegance and service of a resturant is fundamental to the success of Carl Victor's.

...interfere with the enjoyment of the meal. The decor reflects

...Long Island but is sufficiently modern to attract the young

...light and plants. Brick dividers and a split level layout

...e open center with garden and large skylight provides a

...oom at each table for better table service. The ceilings are

...ns with gayly printed cloth hung loosly between them. The

...eautiful warm affect to the room.

...arl Victor's[2], the lunch menu is specially designed to meet the

... Victor indicates:

...wants a relatively quick, totally delicious and competively

...enu needs to be changed frequently enough so that the patrons

...d but not to often to cause confusion. The cost must be

...the menu must be capable of being prepared the night before

...m of kitchen staff.

[2] Interview with the owner of Carl Victor's, Mr. Carl Victor, Jr., June 1993.

Figure 5 - 1

CREATING A RESEARCH REPORT USING THE MLA STYLE GUIDE

You are ready to begin creating your research report. As you create the report, you will be introduced to the MLA research report style guidelines and the steps to accomplish the settings within *WordPerfect*. The MLA style will appear in *italics* at the beginning of each section followed by the *WordPerfect* settings.

Selecting a Paper Size

MLA Style
A research report is prepared on white, 20 pound, 8 1/2 by 11 inch paper.

WordPerfect **Setting**
The *WordPerfect* default paper size is 8 1/2 by 11 inches. This is the paper size required for the research report. No change to the *WordPerfect* default setting is necessary.

Choosing a Font Size

MLA Style
A research report uses a standard, letter-quality type font in black ink. The report must be printed on only one side of the paper.

WordPerfect **Setting**
The default font type is Times Roman in 12-point font size. This is an acceptable font type and size for the MLA research report. *WordPerfect* defaults to printing on only the front side of the paper. Therefore, no change to these settings is necessary.

Setting the Justification

MLA Style
A research report must be typed using left justification. It is not acceptable to use the full justification option.

WordPerfect **Settings**
The default *WordPerfect* setting is left justification. This means that as you type your report, the right margin is going to move in and out according to the length of the line.

Changing the Spacing

MLA Style
The research report must be double-spaced, including the quotations, end notes and the list of works cited.

WordPerfect **Settings**
WordPerfect allows you to adjust the line spacing of the entire document including the footnote and header areas by modifying your initial code settings. You must change the line spacing in the initial codes area in order to double space the body, the header, and the footnotes of the document.

It is important to note that you cannot change the line spacing of the footnote or the header areas by using the line format option. This format command controls only text within the body of the report. The areas above and below the body of the report are controlled by initial codes command settings. By using the **LAYOUT/Document, Initial Codes Style**, the line spacing of the entire document area can be modified.

To set the line spacing using the initial codes setting:

- Choose **LAYOUT/ Document, Initial Codes Style.**

- When the **Styles Editor** dialog box appears, choose **LAYOUT/ Line, Spacing.**

- Type a number **2** in the **Line Spacing** text box.

- Click on the **OK** button to return to the **Styles Editor** dialog box.

  *The **LnSpacing** code now appears in the **Contents** text box.*

- Click on the **OK** button to return to the document area.

Activity 5.1: Setting the Line Spacing Using Initial Codes

1. Start a new document.

2. Choose **LAYOUT/ Document, Initial Codes Style.**

   *The **Styles Editor** dialog box appears on your screen. See Figure 5 - 2.*

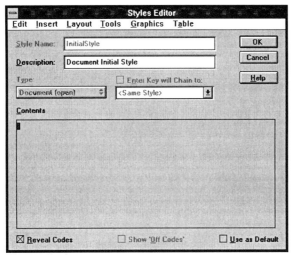

Figure 5 - 2

3. When the **Styles Editor** dialog box appears, use your mouse pointer to choose **LAYOUT/Line, Spacing.**

4. With your insertion point in the **Line Spacing** text box, delete the current selection and type: **2**

   Compare your screen to Figure 5 - 3.

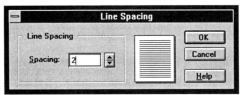

Figure 5 - 3

5. Click on the **OK** button to return to the **Styles Editor** dialog box.

*The **LnSpacing** code now appears in the **Contents** text box. Your completed **Styles Editor** dialog box should look like Figure 5 - 4.*

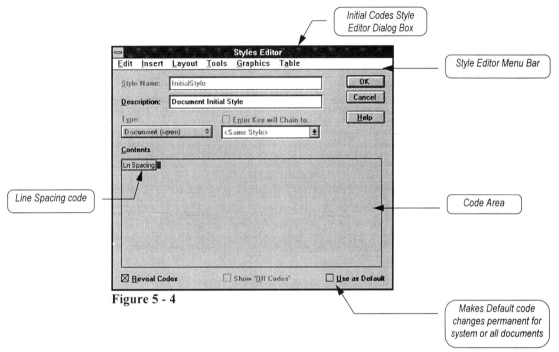

Figure 5 - 4

6. Click on the **OK** button to return to the document area.

Setting the Margins

MLA Style
The top margin of a research report is set at one-half (.5) inches. This setting allows the space needed for the header. The bottom, left, and right margins are set at one inch.

WordPerfect Settings
WordPerfect's default margin settings are one-inch top, bottom, left, and right margins. In order to create this report, you will need to adjust your top margin to .5 inches.

Activity 5.2: Setting the Margins of a Research Report

1. Choose **LAYOUT/Margins**.

2. When the **Margins** dialog box appears, enter one-half (.5) inch as the top margin.

   *Your completed **Margins** dialog box should appear like the one in* Figure 5 - 5

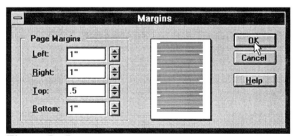

Figure 5 - 5

3.   Click on the **OK** button to return to the document area.

Creating a Header

MLA Style
The research report must have a header that contains the name of the author and a page number. The header information is right justified, one-half inch from the top of the page. The body of the report must appear one inch down from the top of the paper.

WordPerfect Settings

WordPerfect allows you to create both headers and footers. Headers and footers are blocks of text, numbers, or graphics that are repeated at the top or bottom of each page of the report. You can suppress a header or footer code if you do not want the information to appear on a particular page. The header/footer function permits you to create up to two headers and footers on each page.

To create a header for the research report:

*   Move your insertion point to the first page where you want your header to appear.

*   Choose **LAYOUT/ Header/Footer.**

*   When the **Headers/Footers** dialog box appears, choose **Header A** and click on the **Create** button.

*   Click on the **Justification** button on the Power Bar and choose **Right.**

*   Type the author's last name and press the **SPACE BAR** once to move the insertion point to the correct position to enter the page number code.

*   Click on the **Number** button on the **Header** feature bar.

*   When the **Number** pop-up menu opens, click on **Page Number** to insert a page number in your header.

*   Press the **ENTER** key once to insert the necessary space between the header and the body of the report.

*   To exit the **Header** area and return to the **Document** area of your screen, click on the **Close** button on the **Header** feature bar.

Activity 5.3: Creating a Header for the Research Report

For this research report, you will need to select only one header, **Header A**, and have it appear on every page of the report. Because the body of your report must appear approximately one inch from the top of the paper, you will need to enter one carriage return after the header.

1.   Move your insertion point to page one of the research report. This is the first page of the document and the first page on which you want your header to appear.

2.   Choose **LAYOUT/ Header/Footer.**

3.   When the **Headers/Footers** dialog box appears, choose **Header A** and click on the **Create** button.

*A **Header A** feature bar appears on your screen and the **WordPerfect Window Bar** indicates that you are editing **Header A.** Your insertion point is flashing in the **Header** editing area of the screen and your status line indicates that you are at .5 inch from the top of the paper. Look at Figure 5 - 6 to make sure that you are in the correct position.*

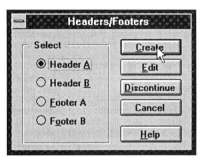

Figure 5 - 6

4. Click on the **Justification** power button and highlight **Right.**

5. Type your last name and press the **SPACE BAR** once to position your insertion point for the **Page Number Code.**

6. To insert the **Page Number Code,** click on the **Number** button on the **Header** feature bar. See Figure 5 - 7.

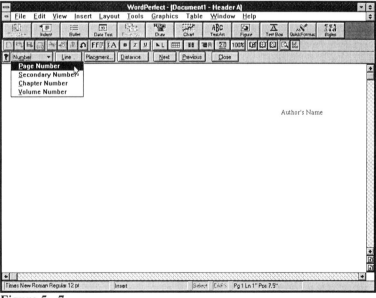

Figure 5 - 7

7. When the **Number** pop-up menu opens, **Page Number** is highlighted. Click on **Page Number** to insert a page number in your header.

    *The body of the report needs to appear approximately one inch from the top of the paper. You must press the **ENTER** key once after you type the header to ensure that the body of the report begins approximately one inch from the top of the paper*

8. Press the **ENTER** key once to set the space needed between the top of the page and the body of the report.

9. To return to the document area and close the header, click on the **Close** button on the **Header** feature bar. See Figure 5 - 8.

*The **Header** feature bar disappears from your screen and your **WordPerfect Window** bar displays the document name. If you are in Page View or Two Page View Mode, your header will appear at the top of each page. If you are using the Draft View Mode, your header will appear only when you print.*

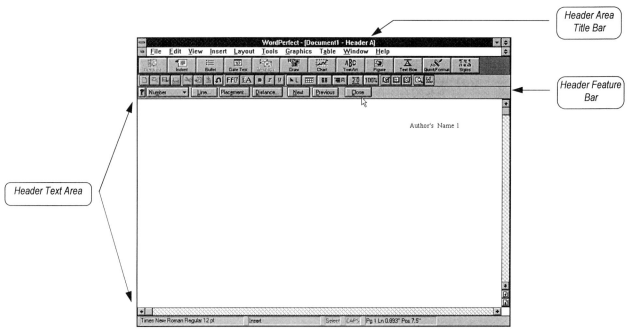

Figure 5 - 8

Creating the Title Information

MLA Style
The research report does not use a title page. The first page of the report contains the title information stating the author's full name, the instructor's name, the course name and number, and the date. The title information is typed one inch from the top edge of the paper.

WordPerfect Setting
You adjusted the distance between your header, which contains your last name and the page number, and the text of the document. Therefore, your insertion point is in the correct position to enter the title information on the first page of the report.

To enter the title information:

- Check your status line to see that your insertion point should be at approximately one inch from the top of the page and at the left margin.

- Enter the title information only on the first page of your research report at the left margin, double-spaced. Since you already changed your line spacing to 2, all you need to do is type:

Author's Full Name

Professor's Name

Course Name and Number

Date

Activity 5.4: Creating the Research Report Title Information

1. Check your status bar to see that your insertion point is approximately one inch from the top of the paper and at the left margin.

    Depending upon the size and type font and the type of printer that is attached to your system, you may have slightly more or less than one inch of space from the top of the page to the top of the report. If your status bar indicates that you are not at approximately one inch, redo Activity 5.3: Creating a Header.

2. The title information is entered only on the first page of your research report and is double-spaced at the left margin. Since you have already changed your line spacing to 2, all you need to do is type:

    [Enter your full name]

    Professor Brian Dorrian

    Introduction to Restaurant Management 101

    [Enter today's date]

3. Press the **ENTER** key once to position your insertion point to insert the file that contains the body of the report.

Entering the Body of the Report

MLA Style
All of the paragraphs begin with a tab, .5 spaces from the left margin.

If a quotation is longer than four typed lines, it must be set off from the body of your text by starting a new line and indenting the entire text 10 spaces from the left margin. The quotation must be double-spaced, without adding quotation marks. If you are quoting only one paragraph, do not indent the beginning of the paragraph more than the body of the quotation. If you have more than one paragraph, indent the beginnings of the paragraphs.

WordPerfect **Settings**
Since *WordPerfect* presets tab stops at every half-inch, pressing the **TAB** key once at the beginning of each paragraph, follows the MLA requirement for paragraphs.

WordPerfect has an indent function that moves all of the text in a paragraph in from the left margin. For this report, all long quotations must be indented 10 spaces or two indent tabs from the left margin. Just press the **Indent** button on the Button Bar twice to indent the paragraph of text.

Activity 5.5: Entering the Body of the Report

You are ready to enter the text of the report. To save time, the text of the report has been saved on your data disk. Place your data disk into your work drive or access the drive where your data files are stored. You will use the **INSERT/File** function to combine a file from our data disk with the document on your screen.

1. Position your insertion point on the next available blank line after today's date in the title information area of your research report.

2. Choose **INSERT/File.**

   Put your student work disk in the appropriate work drive.

3. When the **Insert File** dialog box appears, choose the drive where your DATA DISK is located and highlight the document named **report1.wpd**   See Figure 5 - 9.

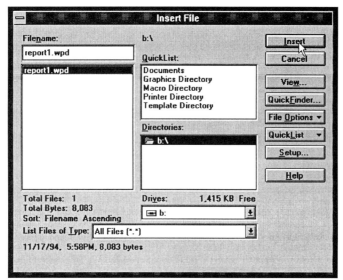

Figure 5 - 9

4. Click on the **Insert** button. When the **WordPerfect for Windows** dialog box appears, click on the **YES** button to insert the file into the current document.

   *The document named **report1.wpd** is inserted into the document on your screen. It conforms to the format codes that you embedded.*

5. Save the document as **report2.**

6. To see how the document appears without printing, choose **VIEW/Two Page**.

   *You are editing a three-page document. When you view it in two-page mode, you will see two consecutive pages at a time. Press the **PAGE DOWN** key to move to the next pages.*

7. To return to the **Page View** mode, choose **VIEW/ Page.**

Indenting Text

MLA Style
The MLA style guidelines require that long quotations of four or more lines appear indented 10 spaces from the left margin. The entire body of the quotation must be indented to the same point.

***WordPerfect* Setting**
WordPerfect's **Indent** function moves a block of text in one tab stop at a time from the left margin. A block of text consists of all characters up to a hard carriage return code.

Activity 5.6: Indenting Text in the Report

For this activity, the researcher of the report interviewed the owner of Carl Victor's, Mr. Victor, about the lunch menu. His comments are a long quotation and should appear indented 10 spaces from the left margin. An easy way to locate a reference to text in a document is to use the **Find** function.

1. In order to locate the reference on page 2, **Mr. Victor indicates**, that will be indented, first choose **EDIT/Find.**

2. Then when the **Find Text** dialog box appears, type a reference to the text you need to locate in the **Find** text box. Type: **Mr. Victor indicates**

3. Compare your screen to Figure 5 - 10. When you are satisfied that your entry is correct, click on the **Find Next** button.

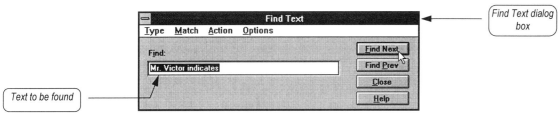

Figure 5 - 10

4. When you have reached the correct reference point, choose to **CLOSE** the **Find Text** dialog box.

5. Remove the highlighting from the text by clicking anywhere in the document area and position your insertion pointer as it is in Figure 5 - 11.

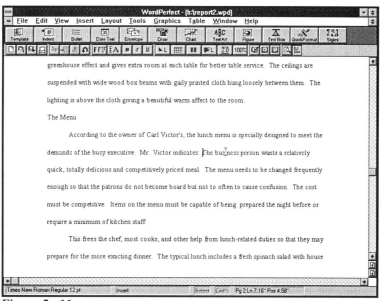

Figure 5 - 11

6. To separate the quotation from the paragraph, press **ENTER** key once.

The beginning of the quotation moves to the left margin.

7. You need to indent the enter body of the quotation 10 spaces. With the insertion point flashing before the quotation, move your mouse pointer to the **INDENT** button on the button bar and click the left mouse button twice.

Your indented quotation should appear the same as the quotation in Figure 5 - 12.

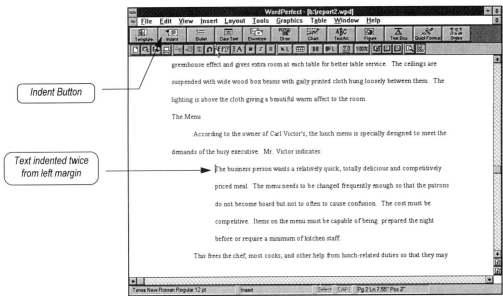

Figure 5 - 12

Footnotes and Word Cited

MLA Style
The MLA guidelines uses two kinds of parenthetical documentation (content and bibliographic notes) and works cited to provide reference to supplementary information about references made within the research reports.

- *Content notes offer the reader comments or explanatory information that the text cannot state. A superscript number is inserted within the text, and the content note appears at the bottom of the page.*

- *Bibliographic notes contain either several sources or evaluative comments on sources. A parenthetical citation is inserted in the research report that refers the reader to the source of the data. The parenthetical citation appears directly after the reference to the work and includes the name of the author, date, and page reference (Jones 1990, 10)*

- *Works cited are the details of the citations and appear under the title **Works Cited** at the end of the research report.*

WordPerfect Setting
WordPerfect has two reference features, footnotes and end notes. The footnote feature allows you to embed a superscript number after the reference within the text ([1]) and moves your insertion point to the corresponding number at the bottom of the page to create the footnote reference. The end notes feature allows you to embed a superscript number after the reference within the

document and moves your insertion point to the corresponding number at the end of the document to create the footnote reference

The default footnote feature in *WordPerfect* is appropriate for creating the content notes required by the MLA style guidelines.

To create a footnote:

- Change to **Page View** mode. Choose **VIEW/Page.**

  *If you are in **Draft View mode** when you create a footnote, your insertion point will move to a separate **Footnote** window. It is strongly suggested that you change to **Page View** when you are creating footnotes. You will see your completed footnotes only at the bottom of your document in **Page** or **Two Page View** mode. If you use the **Draft View** mode you will need to print your footnotes in order to see them.*

- Position the insertion point where you want the footnote reference to appear within the text of the document.

- Choose **INSERT/Footnote, Create.**

- Your insertion point is moved to the footnote area of your document.

- Press your **SPACE BAR** to insert a space before the text of your footnote.

- Type the text of your footnote.

  When you are satisfied with the text of your footnote, click the **CLOSE** button on the **Footnote** feature bar. and click your left mouse button to close the feature bar and return to the document area.

  WordPerfect embeds the appropriate superscript number in the text of the document and a corresponding number appears with your footnote at the bottom of the document.

Activity 5.7: Creating Footnotes

For your research report, you will create two content notes using *WordPerfect* **Footnote** feature. Follow steps 1 through 6 to create the first footnote.

1. Choose **VIEW/Page.**

   To view your footnotes at the bottom of the page you should be using this mode when working with footnotes.

2. Position the insertion point at the end of the first sentence in the first paragraph on page one of the research report. You will place a footnote superscript character after the reference ***Businessperson's Lunch.***

   You are going to insert a content footnote superscript character after Businessperson's Lunch and explain this reference at the bottom of the page. See Figure 5 - 13.

3. Choose **INSERT/Footnote, Create.**

   *Your insertion point is moved to the footnote area of your document and a **Footnote** feature bar is added to your screen.*

4. Press your **SPACE BAR** to insert a space before the text of your footnote.

   To enter the text of your footnote, type:

   A businessperson's lunch is a quick lunch that is specially priced to attract a particular type of patron.

Footnote Title Bar

Footnote Feature Bar

Footnote superscript
number embedded in text

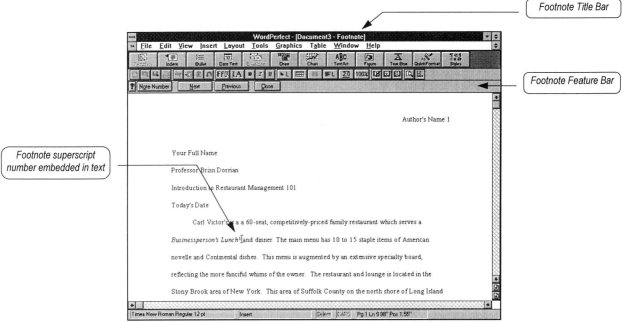

Figure 5 - 13

5. When you are satisfied with the text of your footnote, click on the **CLOSE** button on the **Footnote** feature bar and click your left mouse button to close the feature bar and return to the document area. See Figure 5 - 14.

Footnote Title Bar

Footnote Feature Bar

Footnote superscript number

Footnote

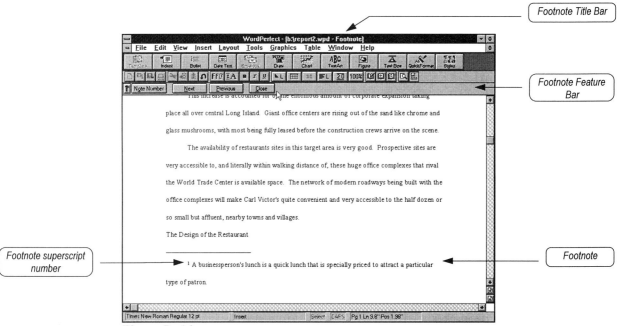

Figure 5 - 14

Now follow steps 1 through 5 to create the second footnote.

1. Position the insertion point on page 2 of the research report after the reference *According to the owner of Carl Victor's*

   You are going to create a content footnote to explain this reference at the bottom of the page.

2. Choose **INSERT/Footnote, Create.**

   Your insertion point is moved to the footnote area of your document.

3. Press your **SPACE BAR** to insert a space before the text of your footnote.

4. To enter the text of your footnote, type:

   Interview with the owner of Carl Victor's Mr. Carl Victor, Jr., June 1993.

5. When you are satisfied with the text of your footnote, click on the **CLOSE** button on the **Footnote** feature bar to return to the document area.

   WordPerfect embeds the appropriate superscript number in the text of the document and a corresponding number appears with your footnote at the bottom of the document. See Figure 5 - 15.

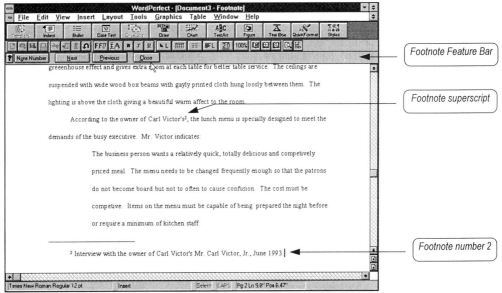

Figure 5 - 15

Creating the Works Cited

The MLA Guidelines
The bibliographic note is inserted at the point of reference. It contains the reference and the page number and is surrounded by parenthesis. All of the works referred to in the research paper appear in an alphabetical listing on a new page at the end of the document.

WordPerfect Settings
WordPerfect has a **LAYOUT** button bar that will help you create the *Works Cited.*

Activity 5.8: Displaying the Layout Button Bar

The references in the Works Cited area of your research document must be prepared using hanging indents. The hanging indent feature can be accessed easily by changing to the **Layout** button bar. *WordPerfect* provides a choice of 15 different button bars which are available to help you format different types of documents. The default button bar is called the **WordPerfect button bar**. You can easily change button bars by performing the following steps:

1. Point to any button on the button bar.

2. Click on the right mouse button to display the **QuickMenu**.

3. Click on **LAYOUT** in the **QuickMenu**.

    The Layout button bar will appear on the top of your screen. This button bar will look like the one in Figure 5 - 16.

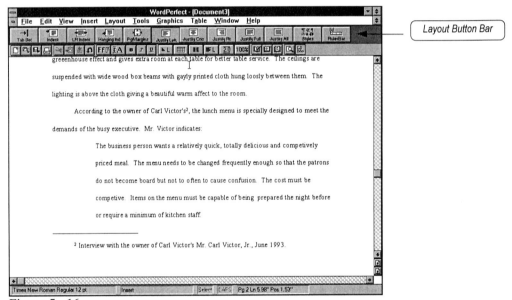

Figure 5 - 16

Activity 5.9: Creating a Bibliographic Note

1. Move to the end of the first paragraph on the first page. Place your insertion point after the sentence that ends *annual gross incomes of $60,000 or over*.

2. To enter the Bibliographic Note, type (**US Bureau of Census 1990, 320**)

    Compare your document to Figure 5 - 17.

Activity 5.10: Creating the Works Cited

1. Hold down the **CTRL** key and tap the **END** key to move to the bottom of the last page of the document.

2. Since the Works Cited must appear on a new page at the end of the document, hold the **CTRL** key and press the **ENTER** key to insert a hard page break code and open a new page.

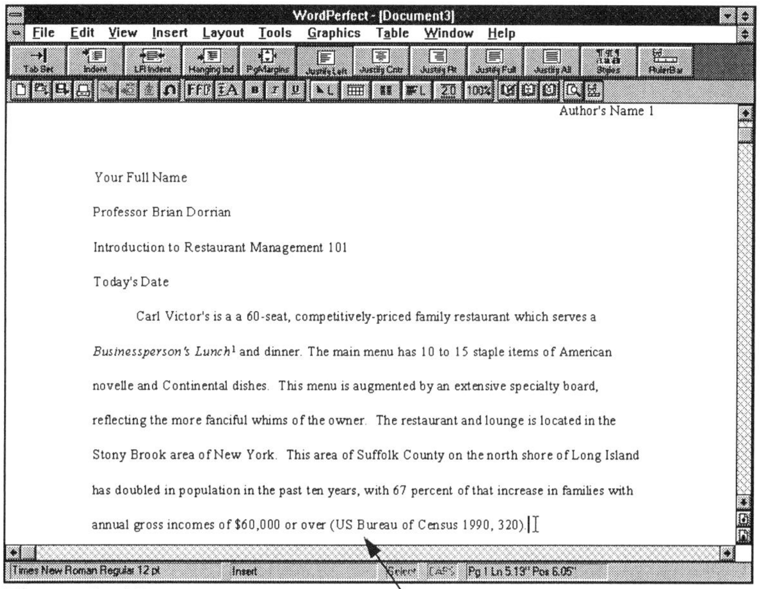

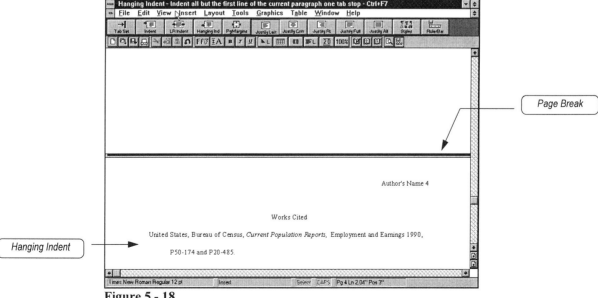

Figure 5 - 17

3. Center the heading **Works Cited.**

4. Press the **ENTER** key twice

5. The document contains only one reference. The reference must be typed beginning at the left margin with the second line indented one-half inch. *WordPerfect* has a handing indent function that does this automatically.

6. Press the **Hanging Indent** button on the button bar and type:

   United States Bureau of Census, *Current Population Reports, Employment and Earnings* 1990, P50-174 and P20-485.

   Your completed reference should look like Figure 5 - 18.

Figure 5 - 18

7. To return to the **WordPerfect** button bar, move the mouse pointer to button bar area, press the right mouse button, and choose **WordPerfect**.

Creating a Graphic

MLA Style

Place illustrations close to the part of the text they describe. Illustration should have a caption which contains the reference Figure and a corresponding number.

WordPerfect **Settings**

WordPerfect has an easy to use **Graphics** feature that allows you to integrate images, lines, and borders within your document. A graphic improves the clarity of your report and the reader better visualizes your message.

WordPerfect allows you to select one of its ClipArt images or import a variety of images from other drawing, painting packages. *WordPerfect* will also allow you to import an image from most scanning programs.

Types of Graphic Files Used by *WordPerfect* in Graphic Boxes

All graphic files are assigned an extension to indicated the type of file. Refer to Figure 5 - 19 for the kinds of graphic images you can include in your *WordPerfect* documents.

Graphic Type	Filename.Extension
WordPerfect Graphic	*.wpg
Encapsulated Postscript	*.eps
Tagged Image Format	*.tif
Designer	*.drw
Lotus PIC	*.pic
Bitmaps	*.bmp
Computer Graphics Metafiles	*.cgm

Figure 5 - 19

Types of Graphic Boxes

Word Perfect has eight different graphics box styles. Examine Figure 5 - 20 to better understand the box's type, typically use, and style.

To create a graphic:

• Place your mouse pointer to the correct position in your document.

• Choose **GRAPHIC/Figure.**

• When the **Insert Image** dialog box appears, select the image that you want to use in your document by highlighting its name.

• Click on the **OK** button to close the dialog box and return to the document.

Graphic Box Type	Uses	Style Description
Text	Quotes, sidebars, or other text. Use to set off information from the body of the document.	Thick line at the top and bottom of the box, anchored to a paragraph.**
Equation	Mathematical, scientific, or business formulas or expressions.	No border or fill, anchored to a paragraph**
Table	Mathematical, scientific, or business formulas or expressions.	No borders or fill, anchored to a paragraph.**
User	ClipArt images, drawings, charts, equations, or tables.	No border or fill, anchored to a paragraph.**
Button	Text, ClipArt images, or drawings. Use to graphically document keystrokes, a push button, or an icon in your document.	Single line border with button fill, anchored to a character.***
Watermark	An image printed as background to the text in a document.	No border or fill, anchored to the page.*
Inline Equation	An equation or expression that is inserted in a line of text.	No border or fill, anchored to a character.***

*Page anchor means its location is related to the top and left edges of a page.
**Paragraph anchor means its location is related to a paragraph.
***Character anchor means that its location is related to a character. The box acts just like any other character.

Figure 5 - 20

Activity 5.11: Creating a Graphic

You need to insert a graphic to be used as the company logo into the text of your research report.

1. Move your mouse pointer to page 3 of the research report.

2. Place the insertion point after the last word of the paragraph that describes the company logo. See Figure 5 - 21

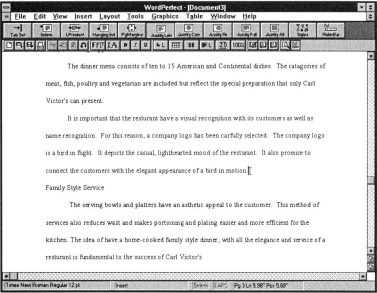

Figure 5 - 21

3.   Choose **GRAPHIC/Figure.**

4.   When the **Insert Image** dialog box appears, highlight the filename **CRANE_I.WPG**.

*Your screen should look like Figure 5 - 22. The graphic filenames are in alphabetic order. You will need to move down through the box to highlight the file **crane_i.wpg**.*

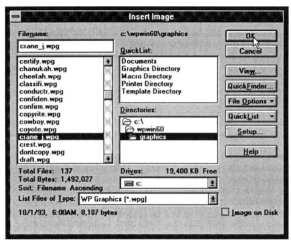

Figure 5 - 22

5.   Click on the **OK** button to close the dialog box and return to the document area.

*A **Graphic Feature** bar is added to your screen, and the graphic is inserted within the text area in a figure box. The graphic is surrounded by eight small boxes called handles. When the handles are surrounding the box this means the box is selected and you can perform alterations to the box such as move, resize, or delete. If the handles are not showing, the graphic box is not selected. To select a graphic box, move your insertion point inside the box, and click your left mouse button. To deselect a graphic box, move your insertion point outside the box and click anywhere in the document area.*

Activity 5.12: Creating a Caption for the Graphic Box

1.   Make sure your graphic box is selected. The handles must be showing.

2.   From the **Graphic Feature** bar select **Caption.** See Figure 5 - 23.

3.   When the **Box Caption** box appears, choose **Edit.** See Figure 5 - 24.

4.   The dialog box will disappear from your screen and your insertion point is flashing next to Figure 1.

5.   Press the **SPACE BAR** once after **Figure** 1 and type: **Company Logo**

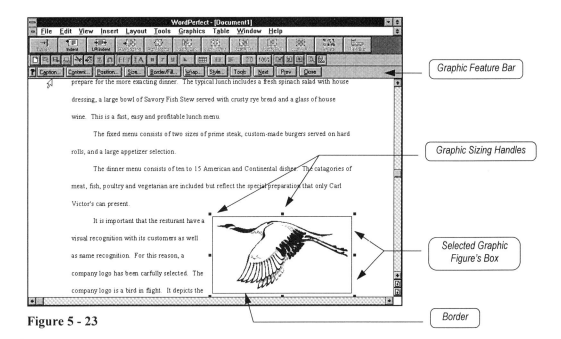

Graphic Feature Bar

Graphic Sizing Handles

Selected Graphic Figure's Box

Border

Figure 5 - 23

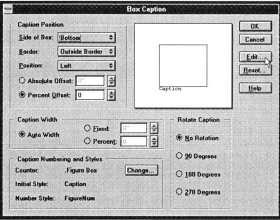

Figure 5 - 24

4. To close the caption and return to the document, click on the **Close** button on the **Graphic Feature** bar. See Figure 5 - 25.

    When you close the caption and return to the document the handles are removed from around the graphic box leaving just the line border.

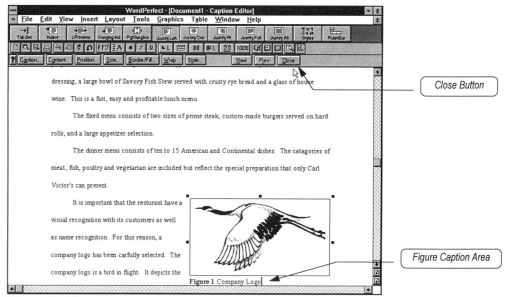

Figure 5 - 25

Finishing your document

Your completed document should look like Figure 5 - 1. You must do a spell check, save your document as **report2,** and print a copy for your instructor.

KEY TERMS

Bibliographic Notes	Graphic
Citation	Header
Content Notes	Initial Codes Style
End Notes	Insert File
Find Text	Resizing The Graphic
Footnote	Works Cited

INDEPENDENT PROJECTS

Independent Project 5.1: Entering a Footnote and Work Cited

1. Open the **report2.wpd** document.

2. Using the **EDIT/Find** function, locate the reference to Savory Fish Stew on page 3.

3. Position your insertion point after the reference and insert a footnote code.

4. Type the following text for the content footnote:

   A wonderful blend of white fish, vegetables, and ginger sauce.

5. Move your insertion point to the last page of the research report and add a reference using the hanging indent function. Remember that the Work Citations are to appear in alphabetic order.

    Rudkin, Margaret, *The Margaret Rudkin Pepperidge Farm Cookbook*,   Galahad Books, 1963.

Independent Project 5.2: Moving the Graphic Box

1. Open the **report2.wpd** document.

2. Position the mouse pointer within the company logo graphic box, and click to select the box. Your mouse pointer should now appear as a four headed arrow.

3. Drag the mouse pointer by holding down the left mouse button and moving the box to its new location which is on the left side of the paragraph.

4. Release the mouse button.

    Your graphic should be positioned in the same way as the graphic in the Figure 5 - 26.

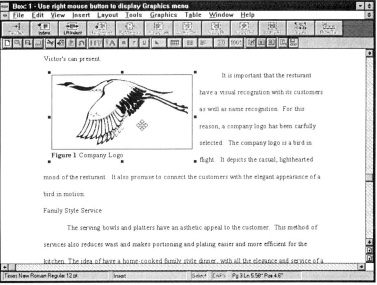

Figure 5 - 26

Independent Project 5.3: Resizing the Graphic Box

To change the size of a graphic box you can select **Size** from the **Graphic Feature** bar or use the mouse. The mouse is generally faster and easier. If all of your graphic boxes need to be a certain size, you can use the **Size** feature.

1. Open the **report2.wpd** file.

2. Make sure that your graphic box is selected. The handles must be showing.

3. Move the mouse pointer to the bottom right handle. A double-headed arrow appears.

4. Hold down the left mouse button and drag the graphic handle to the left to resize the graphic box. You will be making the box smaller. See Figure 5 - 27.

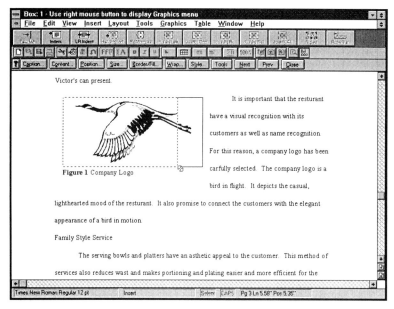

Figure 5 - 27

5. Release the mouse button when you are satisfied with the size of the box.

6. Save the document as **report3.wpd** and print the report.

Merging

Objectives:

In this lesson you will learn how to:

- Create a data file.
- Create a form file.

- Create a letterhead.
- Merge documents.

PROJECT: THE MERGE DOCUMENT

WordPerfect for Windows has a powerful merge feature that allows you to tailor the production of letters, memos, phone lists, forms, and other merge documents. The merge process permits you to send your message to an entire group or a select group of people on the mailing list. Compare the messages below and decide which message would be of more interest to the reader?

Message One
Dear Client: Come join us for a cooking class.

Message Two
Dear Brenda: You really enjoy Chinese cooking and we have a new Chinese cooking class coming up in the Fall. Why not join us?

Message One is a standard sales letter. Message Two addresses the reader, Brenda, and ties her interest in food to the current class offerings. This message is more like a personal invitation to join the class.

The President of Creative Cookery, Brian Dorrian, wants you to send a personalized, block style letter to each client about the fall cooking classes. Your job is to create the *data file* of clients' names and addresses and merge it with a *form file* that contains Brian's message.

The merge process has three parts. In Part 1, you create a *data file* that contains the individualized information about your clients. In Part 2, you create a *form file* that contains the design/format of the letter and the message regarding the upcoming cooking classes. In Part 3, you combine the *data file* and the *form file* using the merge function so that each of your clients receives a similar but unique message. Examine Figure 6 - 1 which contains the three parts of the merge project you will create in this lesson.

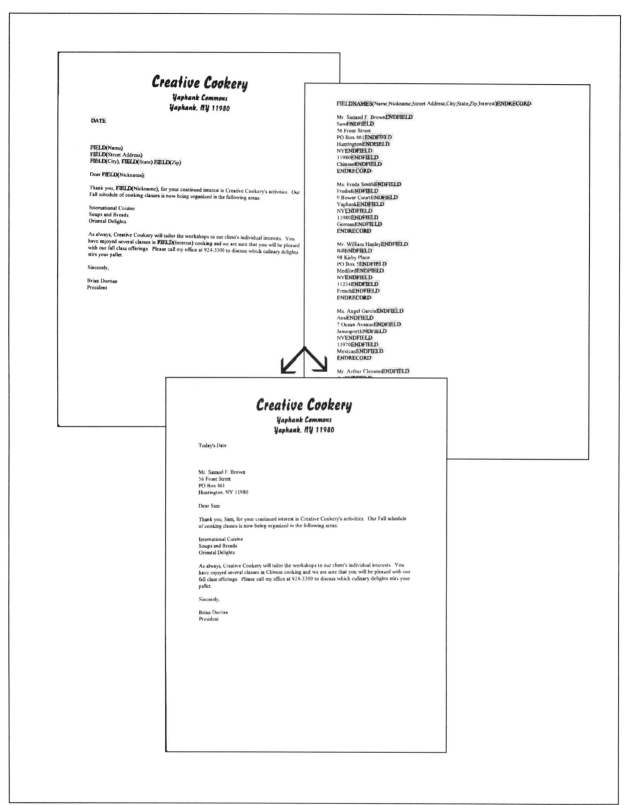

Figure 6 - 1

PART 1: THE DATA FILE

What Is a Data File?

The *data file* is a group of records that contain the individualized information about your clients in a series of named fields. *WordPerfect* allows you to create two types of data files: a *data text file* and a *data table file*. For this project you will create a data text table.

The Data Text File

If you choose to create the *data text file* type of data file, you can have a maximum of 255 named fields and 65,535 records. Figure 6 - 2 displays part of the data text file, **clients.wpd**, which you will create in this project.

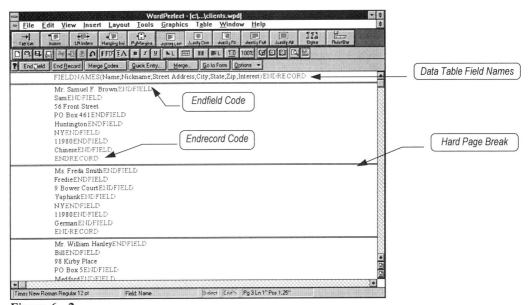

Figure 6 - 2

WordPerfect begins the data file with a **FIELDNAMES** command that details the structure of your data file. The **FIELDNAMES** command ends with an **ENDRECORD** command and a hard page break (a double horizontal line). The data file consists of a record for each client. Each record ends with an **ENDRECORD** command and a hard page break. A record is a series of fields that contain the personalized information about your clients or their **variable information**. A field can contain a single piece of information, such as the client's **Nickname**, or several lines of information, such as the **Street Address**. Each field ends with an **ENDFIELD** command.

The Data Table File

If you choose a *data table file* type of data file, you can have a maximum of 64 fields and 65,535 records. Each cell of the table represents a field, and each row shows a new record. Figure shows the design of a data table file.

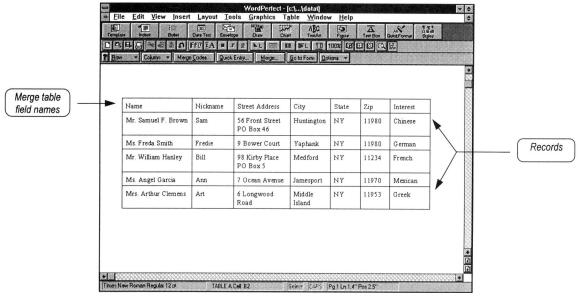

Figure 6 - 3

Creating the Data Text File

As you know, for this project you will create a *data text file* named **clients.wpd**. This file will contain five records, one for each client. The records will have seven fields: **Name, Nickname, Street Address, City, State, Zip, Interest.** You will fill the fields with the unique information about your clients; that is the **variable information.** For example, if the field is **Nickname,** the variable information for one record might be **Johnny.**

It is a good practice to create your *data file* before you design your *form file.* It is important to design your *data file* with as much flexibility as possible so that it is useful not only for this project but for future projects. For example, you should create a separate field for each unique piece of information.

To create a data text file:

- Start a new document.

- Choose **TOOLS/Merge** from the menu bar.

- When the **Merge** dialog box appears, click on the **Data** button. A **Merge Feature** Bar displays on your screen, and the **Create Data File** dialog box opens.

- Verify that your insertion point is flashing in the **Name A Field** text box in the **Create Data File** dialog box.

- Type the first field name for your record and then press the **ENTER** key to move to the **Field Name List** list box.

- Enter the remaining field names to include in your record using the same method.

- When your last field name appears in your **Field Name List** list box, click on the **OK** button.

- The **Quick Data Entry** dialog box appears on your screen. You are now ready to enter your clients' **variable information** into the records.

Activity 6.1: Creating a Data Text File

You are ready to create a data file for the clients of Creative Cookery. You will name your data file **clients.wpd**. It will contain five records each with seven named fields (Name, Nickname, Street Address, City, State, Zip, and Interest).

1. Start a new document.

2. Choose **TOOLS/Merge** from the menu bar.

    *The **Merge** dialog box (Figure 6 - 4), which controls the merge process, should appear on your screen. You will access the **Merge** dialog box for each part of this merge project.*

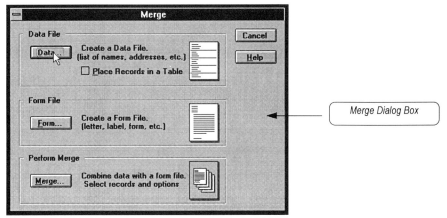

Figure 6 - 4

3. To create the data file, you will click on the **Data** button in the **Merge** dialog box. The **Merge** Feature bar displays on your screen, and the **Create Data File** dialog box opens.

    *The **Create Data File** dialog box (Figure 6 - 5) contains a **Name a Field** text box, a **Field Name List** list box, and command buttons. Be sure that your insertion point is flashing in the **Name A Field** text box.*

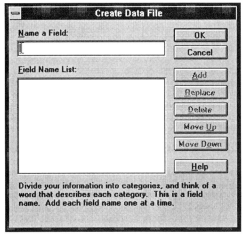

Figure 6 - 5

4. With your insertion point flashing in the **Name a Field** text box, enter the field name. Type:
    Name

5. Press the **ENTER** key to add the field name to the **Field Name List** list box.

    Your screen should look like Figure 6 - 6.

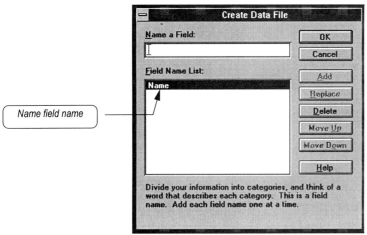

Name field name

Figure 6 - 6

7. Enter the remaining field names in Figure 6 - 7 using the same method as described in steps 4 - 6.

Nickname
Street Address
City
State
Zip
Interest

Figure 6 - 7

8. After your last field name, **Interest,** appears in your Field Name List list box, click on the **OK** button.

    *Your completed **Create Data File** dialog box should look like Figure 6 - 8. When you click on the **OK** button, the **Quick Data Entry** dialog box appears on your screen. You are now ready to enter your clients' **variable information** into your data file.*

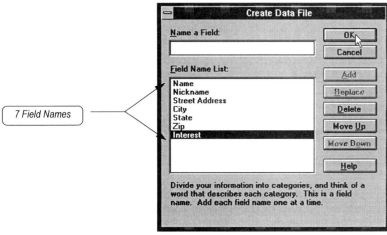

7 Field Names

Figure 6 - 8

Entering Information into the Data File

You are ready to use the **Quick Data Entry** dialog box to enter the variable information about each of the clients into your data file. To familiarize yourself with the **Quick Data Entry** dialog box, examine Figure 6 - 9 which details the parts of the dialog box.

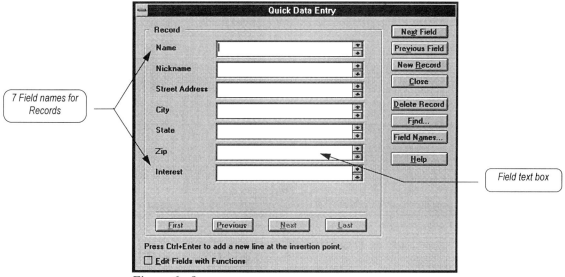

Figure 6 - 9

To Enter Information Using the Quick Data Entry Dialog Box

- Position your insertion point in the first field text box within the **Quick Data Entry** dialog box and type the appropriate piece of variable information for that field.

- Click on the **Next Field** to advance the insertion point to the next field text box.

  *If a field contains more than one line of information, hold the **CTRL** key and press the **ENTER** key to add a new line at the insertion point. Type the next line of information. If you want to view the previous line, position your mouse pointer on the up arrow and click on your left mouse button.*

- Continue this process until all the variable information is complete for this record.

- When you complete the last field of the record, click on the **New Record** button.

  This saves the record to the data file and displays a new record.

- When you complete the last record, click on the **Close** button.

  *This closes the **Quick Data Entry** dialog box and opens the **WordPerfect for Windows** dialog box, which permits you to save your data file.*

- To save your data file, click on the **Yes** command button.

  *The **Save Data File As** dialog box now appears on the screen.*

- Enter the name of your file in the **filename** text box. Make the appropriate selections to assure your file is saved in the correct location.

- When you are satisfied that the **Save Data File As** dialog box is correct, click on the **OK** button to save your document.

Your completed data file appears on your screen. See Figure 6 - 2

Activity 6.2: Entering Information Using the Quick Data Entry Dialog Box

1. Position your insertion point in the **Name** field text box within the **Quick Data Entry** dialog box and type: **Mr. Samuel F. Brown**

Figure 6 - 10 details the correct position for the insertion point.

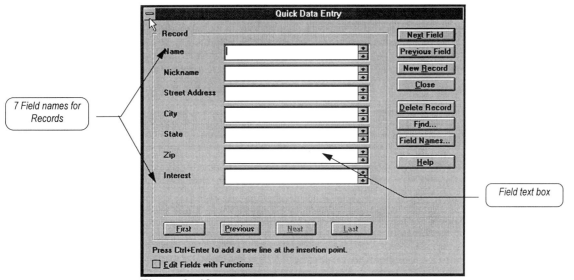

Figure 6 - 10

2. Since this field contains only one line of variable information, press the **ENTER** key to advance the insertion point to the next field text box.

3. Your insertion point should be flashing in the **Nickname** text box. Type **Sam**

4. Since this field contains only one line of variable information, press the **ENTER** key to advance the insertion point to the next field text box.

5. Your insertion point should be flashing in the **Street Address** text box where you want to type the two line street address. Enter the first line of the street address by typing: **56 Front Street**

*This field contains more than one line of variable information; hold the **CTRL** key and press the **ENTER** key to add a new line at the insertion point. Type the next line of information*

6. Hold the **CTRL** key and press the **ENTER** key to add a new line at the insertion point. Type the second line of the street address: **PO Box 461**.

To view the first line of the street address, position your mouse pointer on the up arrow and click on your left mouse button. Your screen will look like Figure 6 - 11.

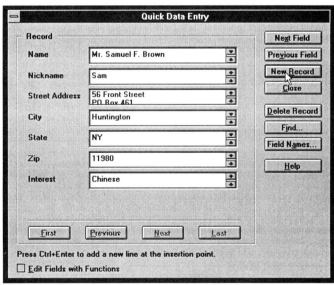

Figure 6 - 11

7. Press the **ENTER** key to advance the insertion point to the next field text box.

8. Continue this process until all of the information for Mr. Brown's record has been entered. Refer to Figure 6 - 12 for the field information you need to enter to complete Mr. Brown's record.

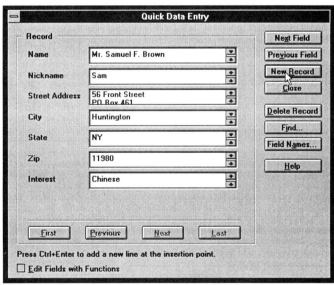

Figure 6 - 12

9. When you complete the last field of Mr. Brown's record and you are satisfied that all of the information is correct, click on the **New Record** button to move to the next record.

The Brown record is now recorded and appears in the background of a new Quick Data Entry dialog box.

10. Refer to Figure 6 - 13 and create a record for each of the client listed in that table. You will create a total of 5 records including the record for Mr. Brown.

Record #	Fields	Client Variable Information
1	Name	Mr. Samuel F. Brown
	Nickname	Sam
	Street Address	56 Front Street
		PO Box 461
	City	Huntington
	State	NY
	Zip	11980
	Interest	Chinese
2	Name	Ms. Freda Smith
	Nickname	Fredie
	Street Address	9 Bower Court
	City	Yaphank
	State	NY
	Zip	11980
	Interest	German
3	Name	Mrs. William Hanley
	Nickname	Bill
	Street Address	98 Kirby Place
		PO Box 5
	City	Medford
	State	NY
	Zip	11234
	Interest	French
4	Name	Ms. Angel Garcia
	Nickname	Ann
	Street Address	7 Ocean Avenue
	City	Jamesport
	State	NY
	Zip	11970
	Interest	Mexican
5	Name	Mr. Arthur Clemens
	Nickname	Art
	Street Address	6 Longwood Road
	City	Middle Island
	State	NY
	Zip	11953
	Interest	Greek

Figure 6 - 13

11. When you complete the last field of the record for Mr. Clemens, click on the **Close** button. See Figure 6 - 14.

*This closes the **Quick Data Entry** dialog box and opens the **WordPerfect for Windows** dialog box which allows you to save your data file.*

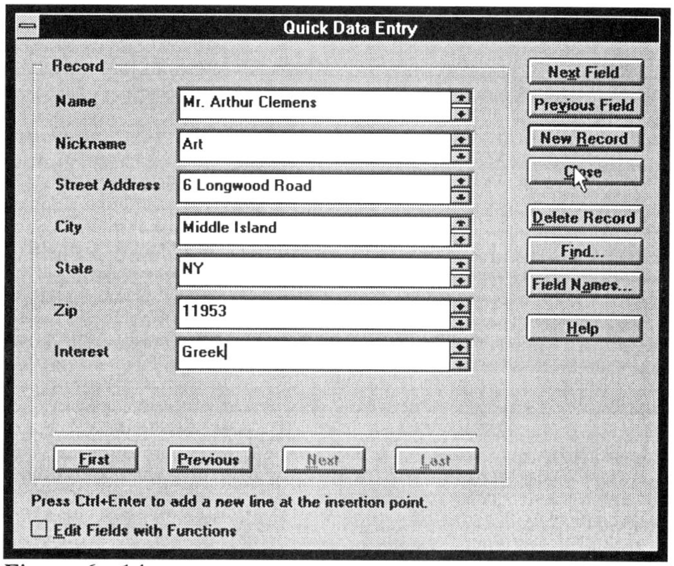

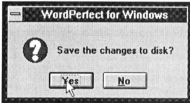

Figure 6 - 14

12. To begin to save your data file, click on the **Yes** command button in the **WordPerfect for Windows** dialog box.

   *The **Save Data File As** dialog box (Figure 6 - 15) appears on your screen.*

Figure 6 - 15

13. In the **Save Data File As** dialog box, enter the name of your data file in the **Filename** text box; type: **clients.wpd**

   *Verify that all your the selections in the **Save Data File As** dialog box are correct. See Figure 6 - 16. You must indicate the location of your data file.*

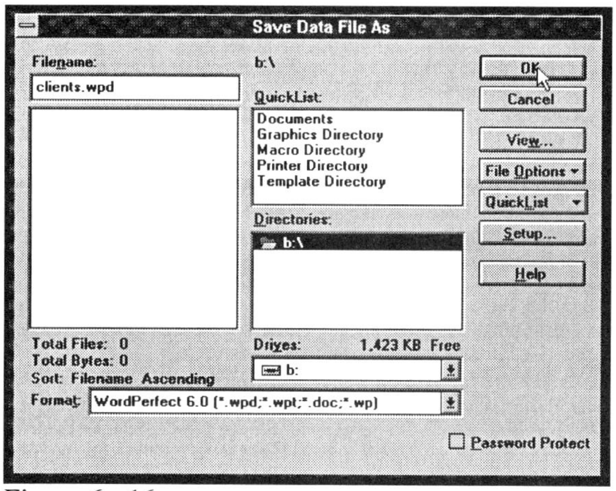

Figure 6 - 16

14. To save your data file, click on the **OK** button in the **Save Data As** dialog box.

*When the **Save Data As** dialog box disappears from your screen, your completed **clients.wpd** data text file will appear on your screen Figure 6 - 17. You are now ready to move to Part 2: The Form File. You can either close the file if your need to stop working or continue working.*

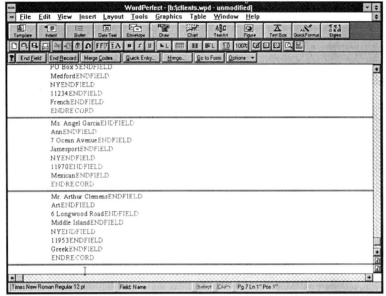

Figure 6 - 17

PART 2: THE FORM FILE

What is a Form File?

The *form file* contains the text, numbers, graphics, and merge codes, which direct the pattern of the merge output. It is the layout or design of the document you will fill with your *data file*.

WordPerfect allows you to associate or connect your *form file* with a *data file*. When you associate your *data file* with your *form file*, you can merge the files to create the merge document.

In this project, you will create a letter and send it to the clients on your mailing list. The body of the letter will include a special reference to the client's food interest and nickname.

To Associate Your Form File with Your Data File:

- **OPEN** the data file you want to associate with your form file.

- Point to the **Merge** button on the **Merge** feature bar and click on the **Merge** button.

- When the **Merge** dialog box appears, click on the **Form** button.

- When the **Create Merge File** dialog box opens, you must verify that the **New Document Window** option button is selected, and click on the **OK** button.

- When the **Create Form File** dialog box opens, point to the **Select File** button that appears next to the **Associate a Data File** text box and click your left mouse button.

- When the **Select File** dialog box opens, highlight the filename of your data file and click on the **OK** button.

- When the **Create Form File** dialog box reappears, the name of your data file should appear in the **Associate a Data File** text box. Then click on the **OK** button to open your form document.

Activity 6.3: Associating Your Form File with Your Data File

You just finished creating the data file, **clients.wpd**, which contains information on each of Creative Cookery's clients. Now you must design the form file that will contain the document's message and the merge codes. You begin the process by associating the form file and the data file.

1. If your data file, **clients.wpd**, is not in the document area, open the file.

   *Your screen should look like Figure 6 - 17, which contains the data file and the **Merge** feature bar. You now are ready to associate the **clients.wpd** data file with your form file.*

2. To associate with your form file, point to the **Merge** button on the **Merge** feature bar and click on the **Merge** button.

3. When the **Merge** dialog box appears, click on the **Form** button. See Figure 6 - 18.

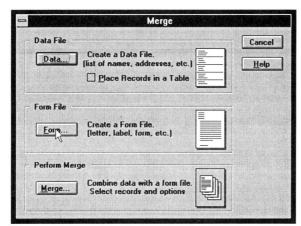

Figure 6 - 18

4. When the **Create Merge File** dialog box opens, you must verify that the **New Document Window** option button is selected, and click on the **OK** button. See Figure 6 - 19.

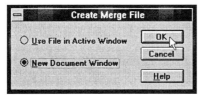

Figure 6 - 19

5. When the **Create Form File** dialog box opens, point to the **Select File** button that appears next to the **Associate a Data File** text box and click your left mouse button. See Figure 6 - 20.

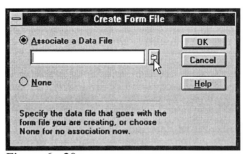

Figure 6 - 20

6. When the **Select File** dialog box opens, highlight the filename of your data file, **clients.wpd,** and click on the **OK** button. See Figure 6 - 21.

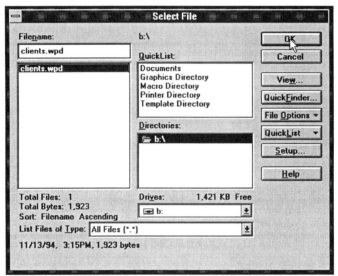

Figure 6 - 21

7. When the **Create Form File** dialog box reappears, the name of your data file **clients.wpd** should appear in the **Associate a Data File** text box. See Figure 6 - 21.

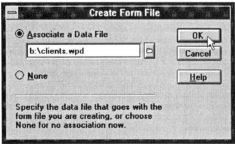

Figure 6 - 22

8. Click on the **OK** button to open your form document.

You have associated your data file with the form file you are about to create. As a result, the information from your data file is available for you to use in your form file.

Creating the Form File

Once the form file is associated with the data file you can begin creating the form file. Type text to appear in every letter in the usual manner. Wherever information will be called in from the data file, insert a *field merge code.*

To insert a field merge code:

- Place your insertion point in the position in your document where you want the fieldname merge code to appear.

- Point to the **Insert Field** button on the **Merge** feature bar and click on the left mouse button. **WordPerfect** opens the **Insert Field Name or Number** dialog box.

- Highlight the field name you want to include in your form file and click on the **Insert** button to include the code in your document.

Activity 6.4: Creating a Form File

Your form file for this project is a letter to the Creative Cookery's clients about new cooking classes. The final document will look like Figure 6 - 23

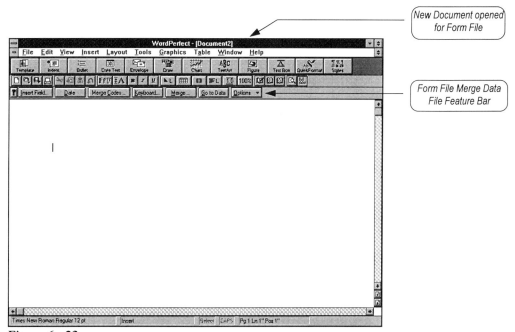

Figure 6 - 23

To create the form file, you must adjust your top margin to one-half inch and create a letterhead. Then you type the letter in block style format that places the parts of the letter including the date, inside address, salutation, body of the letter, and the complimentary close at the left margin. As you enter the letter, you insert the appropriate merge codes to assure your personalized message during the merge process.

1. Adjust your top margin to one-half inch to allow room for your letterhead. Choose **LAYOUT/Margins**. See Figure 6 - 24.

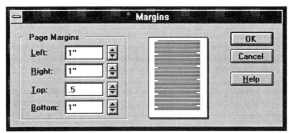

Figure 6 - 24

2. Set Justification to center and type **Creative Cookery**. Select the text and choose the Brush 738BT Font Type and a 36 point size:

Creative Cookery

3. Type the address and then set it in a Brush 738BT Font Type and an 18 point size.

Yaphank Commons
Yaphank, NY 11980

4. After you have entered the letterhead, press the **ENTER** key twice and change Justification to left. Check that your position is at approximately Ln 2" and that the Font Type and Size is Times New Roman Regular 12 points. You are now ready to enter the body of your letter.

    Verify the position of your insertion point on your status bar. You must move your insertion point to approximately two inches from the top of the page to allow for the proper amount of space between the letterhead and your date. It will also center the document properly on the page. Your insertion point should be at the left margin.

5. Move your mouse pointer to the **Merge** feature bar and point to the **Date** button.

    The Merge feature bar appears at the top of your form file. See Figure 6 - 25.

6. Click on the **Date** button to insert a date code in your form file.

    You can type the date at the top of the letter. However, you will want to reuse this letter each time you have a new group of classes to offer. By embedding a date code, you can design your form letter so that the date on which the merge occurs is embedded whenever you use the form letter. This is a time saver and prevents errors.

7. Press the **ENTER** key four times to properly position your insertion point for the inside address.

8. From the **Merge** feature bar, click on the **Insert Field** button.

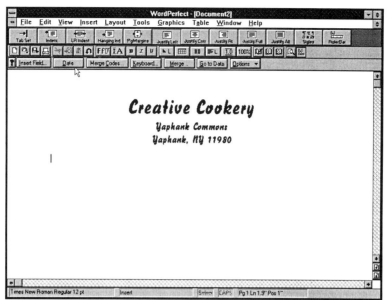

Figure 6 - 25

9. When the **Insert Field Name Or Number** dialog box appears, highlight **Name** and click on the **Insert** button. See Figure 6 - 26.

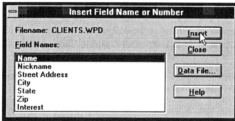

Figure 6 - 26

10. Press the **ENTER** key once to move to the next line of type.

11. From the **Insert Field Name Or Number** dialog box, click on **Street Address**, then click on ***INSERT***

12. Press the **ENTER** key once to move to the next line of type.

13. From the **Insert Field Name Or Number** dialog box, click on **City,** then click on **Insert**

14. Type a comma, and then press the **SPACE BAR** once to the insert the necessary punctuation and a space before the next field.

15. From the **Insert Field Name Or Number** dialog box, click on **State** and click on **Insert**.

16. Press the **SPACE BAR** once to insert a space before the next field.

17. From the **Insert Field Name Or Number** dialog box, click on **Zip,** then click on **Insert**.

18. Press the **ENTER** key twice to leave a blank line before the salutation.

19. Type: **Dear**

20. Press the **SPACE BAR** once to insert a space before the **Nickname** field code.

21. From the **Insert Field Name Or Number** dialog box, click on **Nickname**, then click on **Insert**.

22. Type a colon (:) to close the salutation.

23. Press the **ENTER** key twice to position the insertion point for the body of the letter.

*Your insertion point is now in position to enter the body of the letter using block style format. Type each paragraph at the left margin with a double space separating paragraphs. You will insert two field codes in the text: **Nickname** and **Interest**. Enter the body of the letter as it appears in Figure 6 - 27.*

```
DATE



FIELD(Name)
FIELD(Street Address)
FIELD(City), FIELD(State) FIELD(Zip)

Dear FIELD(Nickname):

Thank you, FIELD(Nickname), for your continued interest in Creative Cookery's activities.  Our
Fall schedule of cooking classes is now being organized in the following areas:

International Cuisine
Soups and Breads
Oriental Delights

As always, Creative Cookery will tailor the workshops to our client's individual interests.  You
have enjoyed several classes in FIELD(Interest) cooking and we are sure that you will be pleased
with our fall class offerings.  Please call my office at 924-3300 to discuss which culinary delights
stirs your pallet.

Sincerely,

Brian Dorrian
President
```

Figure 6 - 27

Activity 6.5: Completing Your Form Letter

Before you can perform the merge, you must **Close** the **Insert Field Name** dialog box, spell check your document, and save your *form file* to your disk

1. From the **Insert Field Name Or Number** dialog box, click on **Close**

   This tells WordPerfect that you do not want to select another field code.

2. Check the spelling of your document. Choose **TOOLS/Speller**

3. Save your form file, choose **FILE/Save.** Then type the filename, **classes.wpd**.

Part 3: THE MERGE

About the Merge Process

Merge is the process of combining a *data file* and a *form file* to create a *merge file*. When you created your *form file* **classes.wpd** you associated or linked to your *data file, clients.wpd*. Your two files are associated and ready for the merge process now and in the future.

To merge with your form file in the active window:

- From the **Merge** feature bar, click on the **Merge** button.

- When the **Merge** dialog box appears, click on the **Merge** button in the **Perform Merge** text box.

- When the **Perform Merge** dialog box appears, verify the information and then click on **OK** to perform the merge.

Activity 6.6: Merging the Form and Data Files

In this project you will combine your *Data file*, **clients.wpd,** and your *form file*, **classes.wpd.** This merge will output to the screen. Your merge document will look like the documents in Figure 6 - 1

1. From the **Merge Feature** bar, click on the **Merge** button

2. When the **Merge** dialog box appears, click on the **Merge** button in the **Perform Merge** area of the dialog box.

3. When the **Perform Merge** dialog box appears, verify the information. It should be the same as Figure 6 - 28

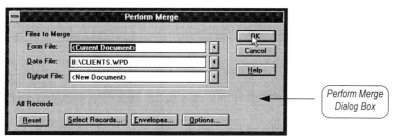

Figure 6 - 28

4. Click on the **OK** button to perform the merge.

    The merge document is now opened to a new document window. You can choose to save and print this document.

5. The letter to the last person in the data file appears. Use the **Previous Page** button on the vertical scroll bar to view each letter created by the merge.

KEY TERMS

Associate A Data File

Create Data File Dialog Box

Data File

Data Table

Data Text File

Endfield

Endrecord

Fieldnames

Form File

Insert Field Name Or Number Dialog Box

Quick Data Entry Dialog Box

Variable Information

INDEPENDENT PROJECTS

Independent Project 6.1: Adding Records to a Data File

You need to add four new clients to your *data file.*

1. Open the *data file* you created earlier named **clients.wpd**

2. When the **clients.wpd** data file appears on your screen, click on the **Quick Entry** button on the Merge feature bar to enter the new records. See Figure 6 - 29.

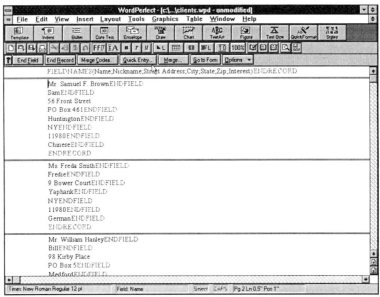

Figure 6 - 29

3. When the Quick Data Entry dialog box appears on your screen, you are ready to enter the four new client records. The variable information for three of the clients follows. The fourth record is for yourself. You should make up appropirate information for yourself. You will need to determine what information goes into which field for each of the records.

Mrs. Samantha Grator	Ms. Frances Farley	Mr. Kevin Grossman
Sam	Fran	8 Terrace Lane
545 Fourth Place	45 Country Club Lane	Yaphank, NY 11980
Selden, NY 11456	Oakdale, NY 11232	Italian
Russian	French	

4. Create a record for yourself and save the file as **clients.wpd**

Independent Project 6.2 Editing a Form File and Letter and Merging

You realize that you need to include a post script (PS) at the end of your *form file* which indicates the cost of the classes.

1. Open the *form file*, **classes.wpd**

2. Move to the bottom of the letter and type the following post script (PS) after the complimentary close of the letter.

3. Save your new *form file* as ***classes.wpd*** and merge with your modified *data file*, **clients.wpd**.

Sincerely,

Brian Dorrian

PS: Our prices for Fall cooking classes will stay at $45. Why not call and register today.

Independent Project 6.3: Merging to an Envelope

You need envelopes for the each of merge letters you created earlier. To do this you will need to create a envelope *form file* and merge it with your *data file*, **clients.wpd**. If you do not wish to print the merge file, you can save it to the disk as **env6.wpd**.

To create an envelope from your merge file:

1. Open **clients.wpd.**

2. Click on the **Merge** button on the merge feature bar.

3. When the **Merge** dialog box appears, click on the **Merge** button.

4. When the **Perform Merge** dialog box appears, click on the **Envelopes** button. See Figure 6 - 30.

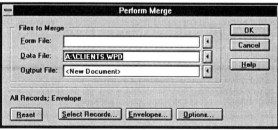

Figure 6 - 30

5. When the **Envelope** dialog box appears, click on the **Field** button to select the appropriate field names to insert into your envelope. See Figure 6 - 31

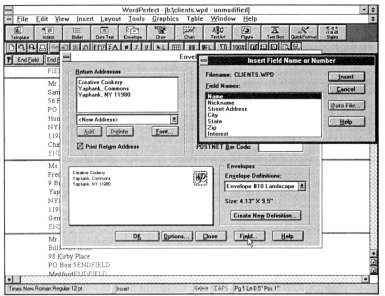

Figure 6 - 31

6. Your completed **Envelope** dialog box should appear as Figure 6 - 32.

   Adjust the font for the return address to complement the Creative Cookery's letterhead, which was done in a Brush 738BT font type, and choose a 12 point font size

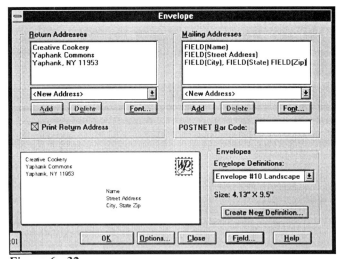

Figure 6 - 32

7. Click on the **OK** button.

8. When the **Perform Merge** dialog box appears, select to your **classes.wpd** as your form file. See . Figure 6 - 33.

9. Click on the **OK** button to perform the merge.

   Your merged document will contain your merged letters with the envelopes at the end of the document.

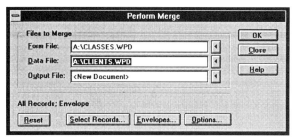

Figure 6 - 33

Independent Project 6.4: Creating Mailing Labels

You need to create mailing labels for all of your clients to send them a brochure of your cooking classes.

To create a mailing label:

1. Select **LAYOUT/Labels.**

2. When the **Labels** dialog box appear, highlight 3M7730 as the label type.

   Note: The 3M7730 is appropriate for most laser printers. If you plan to print the labels, you might need to choose a different label appropriate for your printer.

3. Click on **SELECT.**

   Note: This changes the paper size to label.

4. Select **TOOLS/Merge**, then choose **Form.**

5. When the **Create Merge File** dialog box appears, click on the **OK** button.

6. When the **Create Form File** dialog box appears, associate your data file, **clients.wpd.**

7. Enter the appropriate fields for your label as shown in Figure 6 - 34.

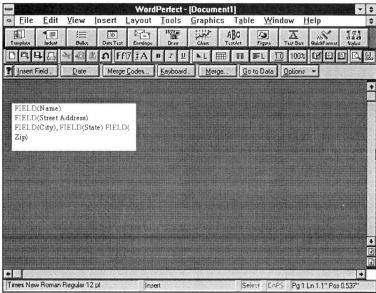

Figure 6 - 34

8. Close the **Insert Field Name** dialog box.

9. Click on the **Merge** button on the **Merge** feature bar.

10. Click on the **Merge** button in the **Merge** dialog box.

11. When the **Perform Merge** dialog box appears, click on the **OK** button.

Lesson 7 Creating Tables

Objectives:

In this lesson you will learn to:

- Create a table
- Join cells
- Enter text into a table

- Justify text within a cell
- Shade cells
- Add a row to a table

PROJECT: TABLES

WordPerfect for Windows has a useful table feature that allows you to improve the appearance of lists, invoices, calendars, and business forms. A table presents information in rows and columns that allow the reader to understand clearly your message. The column separates the information across the table. The row separates the information down the table. The intersection of a column and a row is a cell. *WordPerfect* allows you to have a maximum of 64 columns and 32,767 rows or you can have a total of 2,097,088 cells in your table.

Creative Cookery	
October Calendar	
Workshops	**Date**
Bread Basics	October 4
Soup Starters.	October 5
Japanese Cooking	October 9
German Cooking	October 10
Italian Cooking	October 12
Greek Cooking	October 14
Indian Cooking	October 17
Oriental Cooking	October 24

Figure 7 - 1

In this project you will create the table in Figure 7 - 1, which contains information about Creative Cookery's October workshop offerings. You will learn how to design the basic table, enter text,

159

join cells, and add shading to a cell. You will then edit your table to add a row of information about a new workshop. Your final table will look like Figure 7 - 2.

Creative Cookery	
October Calendar	
Workshops	**Date**
Bread Basics	October 4
Soup Starters.	October 5
International Cuisine Workshops	
Japanese Cooking	October 9
German Cooking	October 10
Italian Cooking	October 12
Greek Cooking	October 14
Indian Cooking	October 17
Oriental Cooking	October 24

Figure 7 - 2

CREATING THE TABLE

Designing Your Table

You can always modify your table after you create it. However, you will save a great deal of time and effort by thinking ahead. Consider the following factors when planning the design or layout of your table:

- Determine the appropriate font type and size to use in your table. The font type and size will affect your column width. It will also determine the amount of text you can fit in each cell and the general appearance of the table. If you select your font before you create your table, *WordPerfect* will size the columns according to the font size.

- Select the paper size and orientation to use. Do you want 8 1/2 by ll inch paper in portrait or landscape orientation? Perhaps you need a larger or smaller paper size. Your choice will determine the size and appearance of your table. If you select the size of the paper before you create the table, it will make your job easier.

- You should set your top, bottom, left, and right margins. This will allow you to create your table within certain borders.

- You need to decide the number of rows and columns in your table. You should allow one row for each block of horizontal text. A horizontal block contains one or more lines of text, numbers, or a graphic. You should generally plan for the maximum number of columns and use the join feature to combine columns when necessary.

To design a table:

- Select a font type and size.
- Determine your paper size.
- Set your margins.

- Establish a beginning number of columns and rows.

Activity 7.1: Designing Your Table

In this project, you will create a table that details Creative Cookery's October Cooking Workshops. The table uses a Times New Roman type font in 12 point font size. You can use the default, 8 1/2 by 11 inch paper size in portrait orientation. The margins remain at the default settings.

Look at Figure 7 - 3, which contains the document you must create and determine the number of columns and rows to plan for your table.

For this table, you will need to plan 2 columns. (The headings are actually in 2 joined columns.) The table has 10 blocks of horizontal text. You will need to plan for 10 rows.

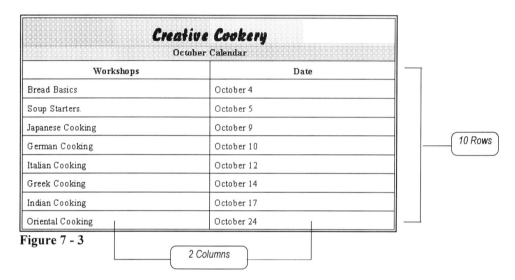

Figure 7 - 3

Creating a Table Grid

WordPerfect allows you to create a table using the menu bar or the power button bar.

To create a table grid using the menu bar:

- Start a new document.
- Verify the font type and size.
- From the menu bar, select **TABLE/Create.**
- When the **Create Table** dialog box appears, use your pointer to specify the desired number of columns and rows.
- Click on **OK** button.

  The table you have designed will appear in the document area.

To create a table using the Power Bar:

- Start a new document.
- Point the mouse pointer to the **Table Quick Create** button on the **Power Bar**.
- Hold down the left mouse button.

  *WordPerfect displays the **table sizing grid**.*

- Drag your mouse pointer to highlight the number of columns and rows in your table.

- Release your mouse button. Your table appears in the document area.

Activity 7.2: Creating a Table Grid

You are going to create the **table grid** in Figure 7 - 4. The **table grid** is the form that you will fill with the information about Creative Cookery's October Cooking Workshops. You will create a table grid with 2 columns and 10 rows.

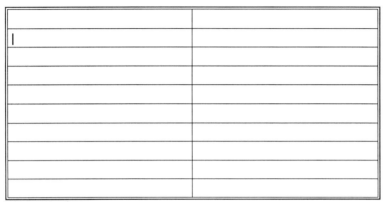

Figure 7 - 4

Using the menu bar to create the table

1. Start a new document.

2. Set your font type to Times New Roman and set the font size to 12 Points.

3. To begin to create the table grid, choose **TABLE/Create** from the menu bar.

4. When the **Create Table** dialog box appears, use your mouse pointer to adjust the scroll arrows on the **Columns** and **Rows** text boxes in the Table Size area or type the appropriate entry in the text boxes. Enter 2 columns and 10 rows for this table.

    *Compare your **Create Table** dialog box to* Figure 7 - 5

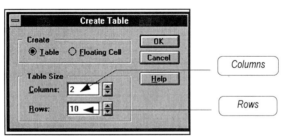

Figure 7 - 5

5. Click on **OK** to display the table you have designed.

Using the Power Bar to create the table

1. Start a new document.

2. Set your font type to Times New Roman and your font size to 12 points.

3. Point the mouse pointer to the **Table Quick Create** button on the Power Bar.

4. Click on the left mouse button.

Word Perfect displays a table sizing grid

5. Drag your mouse pointer to highlight the 2 columns and the 10 rows in your table (2 x 10). See Figure 7 - 6

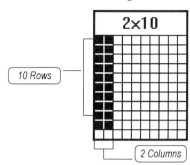

Figure 7 - 6

6. Release your mouse button and the table grid appears in the document area.

ENTERING INFORMATION IN A TABLE

You will enter the information into the cells of the table. A cell can contain text, numbers or a graphic. You can use either the menu bar or the **Table QuickMenu** to modify the appearance of a cell, a column or the entire table. You will know the location of your insertion point within the table by referring to the status bar. In the tables feature, your insertion point is the cell's address or the point of intersection between a column and a row. If you are in the first row of the first column your cell address would be **A1**. Examine Figure 7 - 7 to become familiar with the parts of your table's screen.

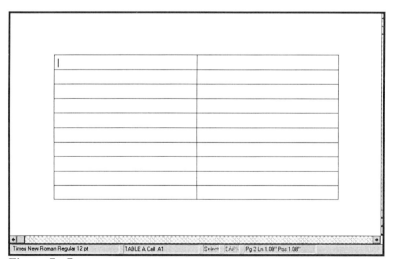

Figure 7 - 7

To join cells in a table:

*   Move your mouse pointer to the first cell of the area to be joined.
*   Select the cells to be joined.

    Move your pointer to the left line of the cell you want to select. At this point, your cursor should change to an arrow. This arrow indicates that you are going to select a cell rather than enter text into a cell. Press the left mouse button and drag the highlighting to the adjoining cell(s).

- Point to the table and click the right mouse button to display the **QuickMenu** and choose **Join Cells**.

To select cells in a table:

- Move your mouse pointer to the left line of the cell you want to select.

  Your insertion point changes to an arrow pointing left.

- Click your left mouse button to select the cell.

  The entire cell is highlighted.

To select a column within a table:

- Move your mouse pointer to the top line of any cell within the column you want to select.
- Click twice on your left mouse button to select the column.

  The entire column is highlighted.

To select an entire table:

- Move your mouse pointer to the left line of any cell within the table you want to select.
- Click three times on your left mouse to select the entire table.

  The entire table is highlighted.

To select a row within a table:

- Move your mouse pointer to the left border of the cell you want to select.

  Your insertion point changes to an arrow pointing left.

- Click twice on your left mouse button to select the row.

  The entire row will be highlighted.

Activity 7.3: Joining Cells in a Table

In order to have the heading Creative Cookery appear across the top of the entire table, you will need to join cells **A1** and **B1** in the first row.

1. Select the first row, cells **A1** and **B1**

    Move your mouse pointer to the left border of cell A1. Your pointer changes to an arrow pointing left. Click twice on your left mouse button to select the row.

2. When the cells are highlighted, press the right mouse button.

    When the **QuickMenu** appears, choose **Join Cells**. See Figure 7 - 8.

To enter text in a table:

- Move insertion point to the correct location.
- Type the text.

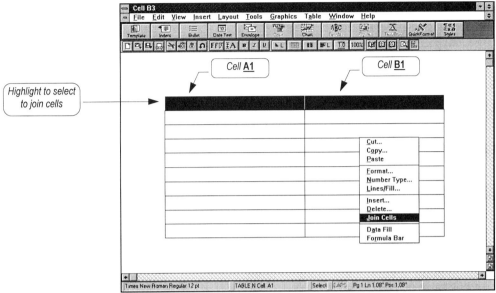

Figure 7 - 8

Activity 7.4: Entering Text in Cells

You are now ready to enter the text of the October Workshop Schedule into the table grid. You need to type the correct text into the appropriate cell. You will then center the headings and shade cells after the text is in place.

1. Place your pointer in cell **A1**.

    You can move the pointer around the table by pointing and clicking. You can move to the next cell by pressing the TAB key. You can move in reverse one cell by pressing SHIFT + TAB.

2. Enter the first line of the heading at the left edge of **A1**. Type: **CREATIVE COOKERY**

    Press the ENTER key after you type CREATIVE COOKERY in order to open a new line for October Calendar, the second line of the heading. Enter the text at the left edge of the cell. In a later activity you will center the text.

3. Enter the second line of the heading in cell **A1**. Type: **October Calendar**

4. Enter the remaining text into the table using Figure 7 - 9 as your guide. Compare your completed work to the figure before you move to the next activity.

Creative Cookery October Calendar	
Workshop	Date
Bread Basics	October 4
Soup Starters	October 5
Japanese Cooking	October 9
German Cooking	October 10
Italian Cooking	October 12
Greek Cooking	October 14
Indian Cooking	October 17
Oriental Cooking	October 24

Figure 7 - 9

Activity 7.5: Centering Text in a Cell

You are going to center the text for the heading in the first row and center the column headings above the columns. When you complete this activity, your table will look like Figure 7 - 10.

Creative Cookery October Calendar	
Workshop	Date
Bread Basics	October 4
Soup Starters	October 5
Japanese Cooking	October 9
German Cooking	October 10
Italian Cooking	October 12
Greek Cooking	October 14
Indian Cooking	October 17
Oriental Cooking	October 24

Figure 7 - 10

1. Select cell **A1**

2. Press the right mouse button. When the **QuickMenu** appears, choose **Format**

3. When the **Format** dialog box appears, choose the **Cell** option.

   *The contents of the **Format** dialog box change depending on which option is highlighted.*

4. In the **Alignment** area, adjust the **Justification** drop down list to select **Center.**

5. Click on the **OK** button to apply the justification.

6. Select the column headings and center them.

Activity 7.6: Enhancing Text in a Table

You need to adjust the font size and type of your heading Creative Cookery and bold the column headings. Your table should look like Figure 7 - 11 when you complete this activity. Using the enhancement features you learned in Lesson 3, perform the following:

1. Change the font's size and type of the first line of the heading **Creative Cookery** to Brush 738BT in 24 point font size.

2. Bold the headings, **October Calendar**, **Workshop** and **Date.**

Creative Cookery October Calendar	
Workshop	**Date**
Bread Basics	October 4
Soup Starters	October 5
Japanese Cooking	October 9
German Cooking	October 10
Italian Cooking	October 12
Greek Cooking	October 14
Indian Cooking	October 17
Oriental Cooking	October 24

Figure 7 - 11

To shade a cell or cells:

- Select the cell or cells to be shaded.

- Press the right mouse button. When the **QuickMenu** appears, choose **Lines/Fill.**

- When the **Tables Line/Fill** dialog box appears, move your mouse pointer to the **Fill Options** area and click on the **Fill Style** button.

- A palette of shading styles appears in the **Fill Options** area, choose the appropriate fill.

- Click on the **OK** button to shade the cell.

Activity 7.7: Shading Text in the Cell

You need to add shading or fill to the heading area of your table. The table function allows you to control the amount of fill within a cell using the **Table Fill/Lines** option. Your table will look like the one in Figure 7 - 12 when you complete this activity.

Creative Cookery	
October Calendar	
Workshops	Date
Bread Basics	October 4
Soup Starters.	October 5
Japanese Cooking	October 9
German Cooking	October 10
Italian Cooking	October 12
Greek Cooking	October 14
Indian Cooking	October 17
Oriental Cooking	October 24

Figure 7 - 12

1. Select the cell **A1**.

2. Press the right mouse button. When the **QuickMenu** appears, choose, **Lines/Fill**

3. When the **Tables Line/Fill** dialog box appears, move your mouse pointer to the **Fill Options** area and click on the **Fill Style** button.

4. A palette of shading styles appears in the **Fill Options** area, choose **10% Fill** (Figure 7 - 13).

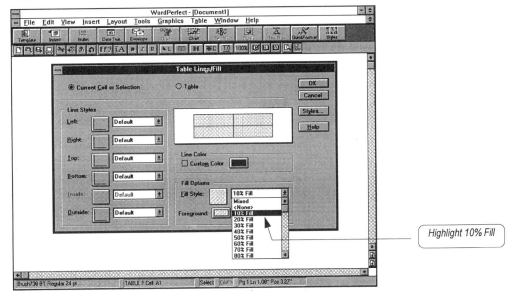

Figure 7 - 13

5. Click on the **OK** button to shade the cell.

6. Save your document as **table1**

7. Print your document.

Activity 7.8: Adding a Row to a Table.

You realize after you save and print your document that you need to add a column heading over the International Cooking Workshops. You will need to insert a row before the International cooking workshops and join the cells to allow the heading to appear across the two columns.

1. Position your insertion point in cell **A5**.

2. Choose **TABLE/Insert**.

3. When the **Insert Columns/Rows** dialog box appears, move your mouse pointer to the **Insert** area and highlight the **Rows** option.

4. Then move your mouse pointer to the **Placement** area and highlight the **Before** option.

    *Your **Insert Columns/Rows** dialog box should look like* Figure 7 - 14

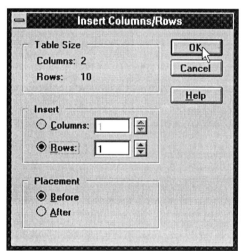

Figure 7 - 14

5. Click on the **OK** button to insert the row.

    The new row is inserted in your table above the row containing Japanese Cooking, October 9. You will need to join the two cells in the new row to make room for the heading.

6. Select cells **A5** and **B5**.

7. Press on the right mouse button. When the **QuickMenu** appears, choose **Join Cells**. See Figure 7 - 15.

8. Enter, bold and center the heading. Type: **International Cuisine Workshops**

9. Save the document as **TABLE2**.

10. Print the Document. Compare you finished document to Figure 7 - 16.

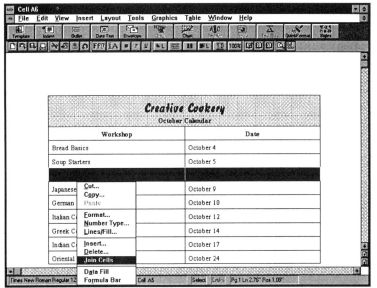

Figure 7 - 15

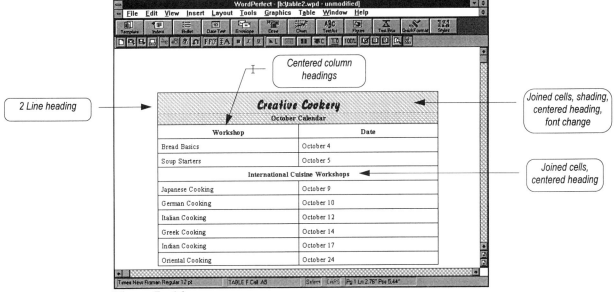

Figure 7 - 16

KEY TERMS

Cell	Shading
Column	Table
Grid	Table Create Button
Intersection	Table Grid
Join Cells	Table QuickMenu
Row	Table Sizing
Ruler Bar	

INDEPENDENT PROJECTS

Independent Project 7.1: Inserting a Row to a Table

You realize that you want to include a special Halloween workshop as part of the October calendar.

1. Open **table2.wpd**

2. Position your insertion point in cell **A5** and insert a row.

   If you need help refer to Activity 7.8.

3. Enter the text as it appears in Figure 7 - 17

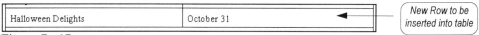

Halloween Delights	October 31	

Figure 7 - 17

New Row to be inserted into table

4. Save your table as **table3.wpd**. Your final table will look like Figure 7 - 18.

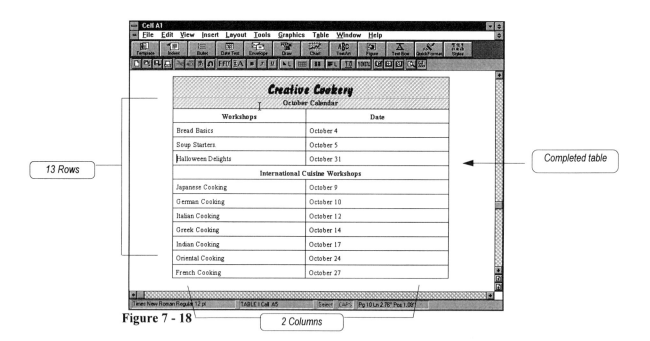

Figure 7 - 18

13 Rows

2 Columns

Completed table

Independent Project 7.2: Editing a Table

You have been asked to create a November calendar of workshops for Creative Cookery. You are told that just the dates and monthly special workshop need to be changed. The fastest way to create the calendar is to open **table3.wpd** and to delete the October dates and the Halloween workshop and type in the November offerings. Save the November calendar as **table4.wpd**. Refer to Figure 7 - 19

Creative Cookery	
November Calendar	
Workshops	**Date**
Bread Basics	November 2
Soup Starters	November 4
Thanksgiving Treats	November 20
International Cuisine Workshops	
Japanese Cooking	November 10
German Cooking	November 11
Italian Cooking	November 12
Greek Cooking	November 14
Indian Cooking	November 15
Oriental Cooking	November 18
French Cooking	November 19

Figure 7 - 19

Independent Project 7.3: Creating a Table

You need to create a table which contains information about the cooking instructors. The table contains three columns and 5 rows. Save the file as **table5.wpd**. Your final table will look like Figure 7 - 20.

Creative Cookery's		
Cooking Instructors		
Instructor's Name	Speciality	Years of Experience
Carl Brown	International	20
William Pope	Breads and Soups	15
John Wong	Oriental	20

Figure 7 - 20

Independent Project 7.4 Adjusting the column width within a table

You have been asked to create a table which includes the description and cost of Creative Cookery's Workshops. To improve the appearance and readability of the table, you will need to adjust the width of columns one and three.

1. Create a table grid that contains three columns and six rows.

2. To adjust the column width, display the **Ruler** bar by selecting **VIEW/Ruler Bar.**

3. Position your mouse pointer on the right border of first column. When the mouse pointer changes to a cross, click and drag the column border until the right edge of the column appears at 2.25 inches. Release the left mouse button. See Figure 7 - 21.

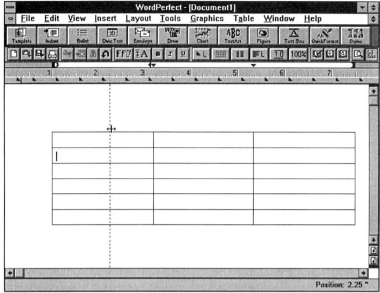

Figure 7 - 21

4. Adjust the left border of the third column to begin at 6.5 inches following the same procedure.

5. Join the cells in the first row to make room for the heading. Enter the text into the cells as it appears in Figure 7 - 22.

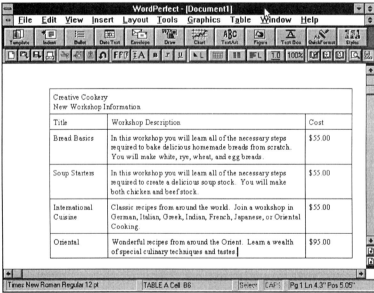

Figure 7 - 22

6. Center all the headings. Set the font for Creative Cookery to Brush738BT, 24 point. The balance of the table should appear in Times New Roman, 12 point. Shade the first row with 10% fill.

7. Save the table as **table6.wpd**

Appendix: Features Reference

The following table contains a summary of the main features presented in the lessons. As you know, most features in WordPerfect for Windows can be performed in a variety of ways. Many of the menu bar commands can also be selected from QuickMenu. Mouse shortcuts involve the use of the power bar, button bar and other mouse techniques. Shortcut keys are keystrokes or function keys. Many features require that the text be selected prior to executing the command. If you need more detail on using these features, the table contains a reference to the lesson describing its use.

Features	Mouse Shortcut	Menu Bar Commands	Shortcut Keys	Lessons
Bold	Bold Button on Power Bar	LAYOUT/Font	CTRL+B	3
Bullet List	Bullet button on Button Bar	INSERT/Bullet	CTRL+Shift+B	3
Copy	CTRL with drag and drop	EDIT/Copy and EDIT/Paste	CTRL+C to copy CTRL+V to paste	2
Double Indent	Drag indent markers on Ruler Bar	LAYOUT/Paragraph, Double Indent	CTRL+Shift+F7	4
Envelope		LAYOUT/Envelope		6
File Close	Double-click document Control Menu Box	FILE/Close	CTRL+F4	1
File Insert		INSERT/File		4
File Open	Open button on Power Bar	FILE/Open	CTRL+O	1
File Resave with same name	Save button on Power Bar	FILE/Save	CTRL+S	1
File Save a new file	Save button on Power Bar	FILE/Save As	F3	1
File Save modified file with a new name		FILE/Save As	F3	2
File Start a new file	New Document button on Power Bar	FILE/New	CTRL+N	2
Font Face	Font Face button on Power Bar	LAYOUT/Font	F9	3
Font Size	Font Size button on Power Bar	LAYOUT/Font	F9	3
Footnote		INSERT/Footnote, Create		5
Graphic		GRAPHIC/Figure		5
Hanging Indent	Drag indent markers on Ruler Bar	LAYOUT/Paragraph, Hanging Indent	CTRL+F7	4

Features	Mouse Shortcut	Menu Bar Commands	Shortcut Keys	Lessons
Header/Footer		LAYOUT/Header/Footer		5
Help		HELP/How Do I	F1	I
Indent	Drag indent markers on Ruler Bar	LAYOUT/Paragraph, Indent	F7	4
Initial Codes		LAYOUT/Document, Initial Codes Style		5
Italics	Italic font button on Power Bar	LAYOUT/Font	CTRL+I	3
Justification	Justification button on Power Bar	LAYOUT/Justification	CTRL+L for Left CTRL+R for Right CTRL+E for Center	3
Labels		LAYOUT/Labels		6
Line Spacing	Line Spacing button on Power Bar	LAYOUT/Line, Spacing		4
Margins	Drag margin markers on Ruler Bar	LAYOUT/Margins	CTRL+F8	4
Merge		TOOLS/Merge	SHIFT+F9	6
Move	Drag and drop	EDIT/Cut and EDIT/Paste	CTRL+X to cut CTRL+V to paste	2
Page Break		INSERT/Page Break	CTRL+Enter	4
Print	Print button on Power Bar	FILE/Print	F5	1
Reveal Codes	Drag bar on vertical scroll bar	VIEW/Reveal Codes	ALT+F3	2
Ruler Bar		VIEW/Ruler Bar	ALT+Shift+F3	7
Special Characters		INSERT/Character	CTRL+W	3
Speller	Speller button on Poewr Bar	TOOLS/Speller	CTRL+F1	2
Switch between document windows	Choose Next Window from document Control Menu Box	WINDOW/Filename	CTRL+F6 for previous document CTRL+Shift+F6 for next document	2
Tab Stops	Tab Set button on Power Button	LAYOUT/Line, Tab Set		4
Table Create	Table Quick Create button on Power Bar	TABLE/Create	F12	7
Table Format	Double-click cell indicator on the Status Bar	TABLE/Format	CTRL+F12	7
Table Insert Row		TABLE/Insert		7
Undelete		EDIT/Undelete	CTRL+Shift+Z	2
Underline	Underline font button on Power Bar	LAYOUT/Font	CTRL+U	3
Undo	Undo button on Power Bar	EDIT/Undo	CTRL+Z	2

Index